Making th

David Richards

Inter-Varsity Press

INTER-VARSITY PRESS
38 De Montfort Street, Leicester LE1 7GP, England

First published 1993

While every effort has been made to trace the copyright holders of all extracts used in this book, the publishers have not been successful in every case. Any amendment to these acknowledgments will gladly be incorporated in future printings.

British Library Cataloguing in Publication Data
A catalogue record for this book is available from the British Library.

ISBN 0–85110–871–7

Set in Linotron Clearface
Typeset by Parker Typesetting Service, Leicester
Printed and bound in Great Britain by
Cox & Wyman Ltd, Reading, Berkshire

Inter-Varsity Press is the book-publishing division of the Universities and Colleges Christian Fellowship (formerly the Inter-Varsity Fellowship), a student movement linking Christian Unions in universities and colleges throughout the United Kingdom and the Republic of Ireland, and a member movement of the International Fellowship of Evangelical Students. For information about local and national activities write to UCCF, 38 De Montfort Street, Leicester LE1 7GP.

Making the connection

To Cathy

Contents

Foreword

So, why another book about Christianity? Aren't there enough already? Yes of course there are and some are better than this one! However the reason I have written this book is to try to show that Christianity really does have something to say to our society and the way we live today. This book concentrates on the basics – the basics of Christianity and how it relates to the basics of life.

For many people the Christian faith seems irrelevant – it's all about a service in a building from another century, sermons in a language from another planet and people who seem to be in a different world!

Yet, across the world, more people are becoming Christians today that at any other time in the past two thousand years. People just like you are discovering the truth that there is a God who wants to make the connection with them. Many people are discovering that if they really examine the Christian faith – not an image that they have retained from years ago – then there is something worth discovering.

Faced with the real issues, there is the realization that God does have something to say. Issues like the need to be loved, loneliness, sexuality, success, death, sexism and suffering. Issues like that bring people to see what's really important in life. There is a need that we have to recognize and express. Remember the Freddie Mercury concert? David Bowie wanted to say something – to express grief, fear, hope

7

and a whole host of emotions. There was no speech, no eulogy, not even a song. But, in front of a stadium of 80,000 pop fans and a world-wide television audience of millions, he simply knelt and prayed the Lord's Prayer. He was making the connection – between God and his feelings.

This book is designed to help you to make that connection. I hope it does. It is the most important connection you will ever make.

A need to live

In the autumn of 1984, one man showed the world its own potential. The shout of 'Feed the World!' became the rallying cry as thousands of people responded to the appeal by Bob Geldof (or, as the media dubbed him, St Bob): 'We want your money and we want it now!' Band Aid topped the charts and churches even used Bono, Midge Ure and Geldof as backing music to their Christmas collections. A raw nerve was touched. So much so that in 1989, a new generation of pop stars used the same song to raise more money for another disaster in Sudan, and reached No. 1 again!

The summer of '85 saw Wembley stadium packed as a succession of superstars from pop music and entertainment drummed home the message to the millions of people watching around the world on television. The pop star Phil Collins criss-crossed the Atlantic in Concorde as the world became united in its support of the millions starving to death in Ethiopia and the Sudan.

Twelve months later, even Live Aid was surpassed. To the beat of 'Everybody wants to run the world', everybody did — or at least so it seemed. Thousands of lives were saved and millions of people were inspired. But one uncomfortable question remained: 'How had things been allowed to get so bad?'

Ordinary people had worked alongside the heroes of sport and entertainment to avert one of the worst catastrophes the world would have experienced. So if there was so much potential for good in the world, how come there was so much potential for bad?

The autobiography of Bob Geldof himself provided a clue. Here was a man whose bravery, honesty, commitment and daring had been the inspiration for millions of people around the world. Yet, as his book showed (and as he had claimed several times himself), he was no saint or plaster-cast hero. Courageously, his book *Is That It?* showed him up, warts and all. He may have the nomination for the Nobel Peace Prize and an honorary knighthood, but the canonization by 'Spitting Image' would be the closest he got to being a saint.

He wrote, 'I don't think I can ever be content, there will always be the push and pull of an eternal, internal conflict, the tiresome civil war that screams on perpetually inside my head, the constant tedious questioning and analysis of motive.'[1]

The paradox found in Bob Geldof is mirrored in the world at large. 'How can there be so much good, and so much bad, in the world?' The writer Alduous Huxley expressed what many of us have felt at one stage or another: 'I am between two worlds. One that is dead and one that can never become.'

Events like Band Aid, Comic Relief, Children in Need and The Simple Truth show us what is possible – the potential for good within humanity. Sadly, the newspapers and television news show us the reality.

For example, in 1975, a plan was proposed at the United

---

[1] *Is That It?*, Bob Geldof (Sidgwick & Jackson, 1986). Used with permission.

Nations to help the Third World. It was a five point plan aimed at raising the standards of immunization, literacy, agriculture, birth control and health education. The cost was to be met by all the member nations of the U.N. and was to be spread over five years. The cost over those five years was the equivalent of the joint expenditure of the then USSR and USA on nuclear arms during the same period. The proposal was rejected.

In 1980, fifty-eight leading countries spent more than $630 billion on military expenditure. The defence budget of the United States alone increased from $143 billion in 1980 to $446 billion in 1989. The cost of one M-1 tank, $2.8 million, is the equivalent of one health clinic in the Third World. The cost of one 524 Apache assault helicopter (used with such accuracy and effect in the Gulf War) is $14 million, which could finance more than 10,000 school classrooms in India. Finally, the cost of one US Navy cruiser would provide 200,000 school children from the Third World with food, clothing and medical and educational care from the time of their birth until they reach the age of twenty! Right wing, left wing, capitalist, socialist, moderate, extreme, fascist, liberal, it doesn't seem to matter. Politics doesn't seem to make things better. In fact, it often seems to make things worse.

It was with some accuracy that a former US Secretary for Defence, Robert McNamara, declared, 'All the evidence of history suggests that mankind is indeed a rational animal but with a nearly infinite capacity for folly . . . He draws up blueprints for Utopia but never quite gets it right.'

An anonymous poet summed up how many people feel as their lives unfold:

> Across the fields of yesterday
> He sometimes comes to me
> The little lad just back from play
> The boy I used to be.

He smiles at me so wistfully
When once he's crept within
It is as though he had hoped to see
The man I might have been.

The dreams of childhood give way to the cynicism and suspicion of later years. As children we all have dreams – mine were scoring the winning goal for Manchester United at Wembley or hitting a century for England to win the Ashes! The reality is somewhat different. In an interview in the *Sunday Times*, the TV presenter and author Melvyn Bragg identified what he called his 'shadow life', that is, the things in his past that he could have been or done.

> I look on my shadow life most days. I think this could have happened, that could have happened – relationships, work.
> It accompanies me. When you're a child, you're 17 people in one day. When my son says to me, 'I'm Superman', he is. As we get older, we settle painfully for the fact that we're fewer and fewer people. Eighteen-year-olds are the best soldiers because they have no conception of death and when you get to the age when you suddenly realise you have a finite life, BANG! you suddenly know the shadow life you've missed.

The past decades have seen people use endless devices in order to avoid the real facts of their lives. We live in a fantasy world of fast cars, exotic holidays and designer clothes. 'Wear this, look like this, drive that, and smell like her' the adverts advise us. Yet the faster we search for the answer, the more the questions multiply. Materially, we can do more, own more, buy more than perhaps any other generation in history. But the facts suggest we are not any happier:

• Suicide now ranks eighth among the major causes of death. It has increased 300% among adolescents since 1960. Our murder rate is horrifically high, yet more people kill themselves than kill others.

• Divorce rates in Great Britain have increased five times since 1960. It is now estimated at 1:3 (in the city of London, it is 2:3). It makes 160,000 children annually the victims of their parents' broken marriages. In 1991, it was estimated that the number of people affected by divorce was one and a half million.

• 37,000 young people were involved in N.S.P.C.C. cruelty cases in 1985. It has also been estimated that 400 children per week are being taken into care in England and Wales alone. The number of calls received by Childline, the telephone help line, although controversial, is surely indicative of something.

• The number of couples living together before marriage was 2% in 1960. By 1980, the figure had reached 21%. In the same year, it was estimated that 47% of girls under 16 years of age had had sexual intercourse. Four years later, the number had risen to 74%. A report in *The Times* on 16th May 1986 asserted that, 'Early sexual activity and an increasing number of sexual partners are undoubtedly important in the rising incidence of cervical cancer.'

Oscar Wilde could well have been writing about our own decade when he surmised that 'Something was dead in each of us and what was dead was hope.' In the search to regain that hope, people have tried various options, either to improve their understanding of life, their quality of life, or the quality of life of those around them.

Some have turned to politics. Even Ronald Reagan, however, was forced to concede that 'Governments tend not to solve problems, merely rearrange them.' Vladimir Illich Lenin, the founder of modern Socialism, confessed on his death bed, 'I made a mistake. Without a doubt an oppressed

13

multitude had to be liberated, but our method only provoked further oppression and atrocious massacres. My living nightmare is to find myself in an ocean, red with the blood of innumerable victims. It is too late now to alter the past, but what was required to save Russia were 10 St Francis of Assisi.'

Science is another option that has been tried. It aims to answer our fundamental questions: How did we get here? Where are we going? How can we explain life? It was the eminent scientist Sir Karl Popper who concluded, 'We do not know where or how to start our analysis of this world. There is no wisdom to tell us. Even the scientific tradition does not tell us. It only tells us where and how other people started and where they got to.'

The pseudo-scientific assertion that we are all a mere product of chance was too much even for Jean-Paul Sartre, a renowned atheist and cynic. 'I do not feel that I am a product of chance, a speck of dust in the universe, but someone who was expected, prepared, prefigured. In short, a being whom only a creator could put here: and this idea of a creating hand refers to God.'

In the search for hope, and an explanation of how we exist, we have to consider the possible existence of God. Millions of people over thousands of years have discovered God to be the answer to their searchings. But which God? Our society offers a variety of choice – Judaism, Islam, Buddhism, Mormonism, Christian Science, Sikhism and Jehovah's Witnesses. Some say God is within, some say he is outside. So who is right, and who is to say? How do we make the connection between God and ourselves? Is there a connection?

In this book we will examine the claims of Christianity. Christianity is unique in several ways. It claims to be *the* way in which God made the connection between himself and his creation. It claims to be the only way that we can really know God. It claims that God came to this planet 2,000 years ago and showed us who he is, and what humanity really should be like. It claims that this God in human form taught about life and death in a way that no-one ever has, before or since. It claims too that this God became so human that he actually died, and then rose again from the dead. These claims are either preposterous, or true. They can be nothing else. Hopefully, as you read the book, the connection will become a little clearer. The choice is yours.

For further reading

Is That It?, Bob Geldof (Sidgwick & Jackson, 1986).
How to Make the World Less Hungry, Kathy Keay (Frameworks, 1990).
The fourth Gospel, John 1:1–14.

─────────────── 2 ───────────────
A need to choose

A sociologist defined the 1980s as the generation of choice. The motto seemed to be 'It doesn't matter what you choose, but that you make a choice.'

Soap operas on television like *EastEnders*, *Neighbours* and *Home and Away* were popular for many reasons, but one of them may well be the number of choices the characters have to make in any given episode. Should a character have kept her baby or have had an abortion? Should Charlene/Bronwyn/Kerry/Matilda marry Scott/Henry/Jo/Herbert? (Delete or add names as appropriate. The characters may change but the plot doesn't.) Does anybody care? They patently do, as the viewing figures indicated and the popularity of actors such as Jason Donovan, Kylie Minogue and Craig MacLachlan showed. One of the reasons such programmes are so popular is that people are able to relate to the choices being beamed into their lounges and living-rooms. They would like to choose like that.

One of the reasons for the success, electorally at least, of the Conservative Party in Great Britain during the 1980s was surely the high priority they gave to choice. The right to choose how children were educated, where and when illnesses were treated, how money was invested and spent, were all part of their manifesto.

The ability to choose is a part of being human. We are built to choose – left from right, right or wrong. Can you imagine a world where no-one could choose? People would be unable to do the shopping because they could never decide what to buy or what not to buy. Motorways would be full of cars and lorries never able to choose which exit to take. Just think of the number of choices that you make in one day – to get up or not, to wash or not, what to wear, what to have for breakfast, cereal or toast, white or brown bread, (granary or plain), cornflakes or porridge, full-cream milk or semi-skimmed, white sugar or brown, orange juice or grapefruit, tea or coffee, caffinated or decaffinated – and all that before you leave the house! In the West, choice is definitely high on the agenda.

Christianity says that as humans we are given a choice. The choice is between a life with God or without God. We are not forced to live our lives as God intends us to or to find out about him. Presumably, no-one is standing over you now with a gun at your head, forcing you to read this book (or, at least, not physically!). So why are we given this ability to choose? In order to find out, we need to begin at the beginning of the story of Christianity.

Perhaps surprisingly, when beginning to examine Christianity, one has to begin with Christmas. Despite the feeling of many people today that it has nothing to do with religion, it really is the place to start – or, at least, the birth of Jesus is.

Christmas does mean different things to different people. Someone has defined it as 'a period of preparations, invitations, anticipations, relations, frustrations, prostrations and recuperations'!

It is undoubtedly a time when we do funny things. We

18

celebrate in December the birthday of a baby born probably in either September or October. We ask children to receive presents from the patron saint of prostitutes! We stick a tree in our living-room and decorate it with lights that never work! It is also the time when jackets all over the country become crumpled and scruffy. The reason? All the coat-hangers have been stolen to make the Blue Peter advent crown! It is undoubtedly too a time of choices.

Young marrieds have to choose: whose parents this year? The shops are full of people making choices: which present to buy; how much money to spend or not to spend; which programmes to watch on television? Choice was also there at the first Christmas.

Mary was an ordinary girl from an ordinary town. In her middle-teens, she was engaged to an ordinary, if poor, man, and her future looked to be mapped out. Then, suddenly, everything was changed. She had a visitor – a very unusual visitor.

The Bible is nothing but honest in the way that it portrays the characters found in its pages. There are no Hollywood face-lifts, or character-lifts. If they stink, you smell them. Mary is described in an ordinary, down-to-earth manner. The writer of Luke's Gospel tells us that God sent a messenger to see Mary. Now the messenger was no ordinary messenger – he did not work for British Telecom, nor was he employed by a Kiss-a-gram agency. From other accounts, he stood at least ten feet high, was identified as an archangel, his body had the appearance of chrysolite, his face was like lightning, his eyes like flaming torches, his arms and legs were like the gleam of burnished bronze, and his voice sounded as if he'd been working in a multi-track recording studio. Imagine if he turned up at your front door! I wonder how you would react! The author of the Gospel is utterly realistic. 'Mary was greatly troubled at his words and wondered what kind of greeting this might be.

But the angel said to her, "Do not be afraid, Mary, you have found favour with God"' (Luke 1:29–30).

The messenger tells Mary that she has been chosen to do a special job for God. But the choice is still hers. She has been chosen because of who God is and not because of anything she has done or said, but the choice to obey God remains hers.

Isn't it amazing to you that the God of the whole universe entrusts the most important job in history to a human being, and depends on her being agreeable to the task?

This is always God's way, however. To force people into following him would not be the act of a loving God. It would be the equivalent of spiritual blackmail, manipulation or oppression. We are not robots or pieces on a divine chess board. It is because God loves us that he gives us the choice to follow him, or not as the case may be. It was no less so in the case of Mary than it is in yours and mine.

Every Jewish girl for hundreds of years had wondered whether she would be the one to bear God's special child. Now Mary was to be that girl. She gave us a model response in choosing to obey God. '"I am the Lord's servant," Mary answered. "May it be to me as you have said"' (Luke 1:38).

So why was this special job necessary?

The clues can be found in the names that are given to the baby whose birthday we are supposed to be celebrating at Christmas.

1. Immanuel (God with us)[1]

The editor of the problem page in *Woman's Own* listed the top ten problems that people write in with. The results are quite surprising. Angela Williams, or Mary Grant as she was known in the column, listed them as:

[1] Isaiah 7:14; Matthew 1:22–23.

20

1. Loneliness – the friendless and unattached.

2. Loneliness – people who feel isolated through having no friends.

3. Loneliness – people in relationships who cannot communicate.

4. Loneliness – people whose relationships have broken down (*e.g.* the divorced, bereaved and rejected).

5. Loneliness – the circumstantial kind (*e.g.* a new house, area or job).

6. Lack of confidence.

7. Marriage and cohabitation problems.

8. Sex.

9. Stress.

10. Family (*e.g.* single parents, step-children, adolescent worries, in-laws, violence and separation).

Quite a list! As Thomas Wolfe has written, 'Loneliness is and always has been the central and inevitable experience of every man (*sic* and woman).' N. F. Calverton meanwhile reasons that, 'Men love because they are afraid of themselves, afraid of the loneliness that lives in them, and need someone in whom they can lose themselves as smoke loses itself in the sky.'

Despite our society being the most mobile in history, more and more people are lonely. They live in literal apartments, cut off from their neighbours, apart from each other. The days when people's front doors were always open are long gone. The separation of the place of work from the place where people live has also been a key factor. Commuters are an invention of this century.

Conversations are now functional, rather than relational. They are for a purpose rather than simply the building up of a relationship or general sociability. Having lived in a city for over fifteen years, my sister finds it strange to return to the small town where we were brought up and to find complete strangers happy to pass the time of day with her on a bus or train.

An illustration of this came in the film *Crocodile Dundee* where there is a marvellous scene in which Mick Dundee, the hero from the Australian outback, arrives in New York. His car stops at some traffic lights. Mick winds down the window and says 'Hi!' to a pedestrian. 'The name's Dundee, Mick Dundee. I'm in town for a few days. Probably see you around.' The bemused pedestrian simply nods. In a city the size of New York, people do not bump into each other! Our society follows the motto of Kierkegaard, 'The crowd is a lie.' Even when we relax, we do so alone. The jogging generation is not one that talks easily to each other, unless it is between deep breaths! Ironically, often the loneliest places to be are at a party or in a pub.

This is not how it was meant to be. As humans we are built for relationships and friendships. We feel hurt when people ignore us or refuse to talk to us. All around us we see the pain of broken relationships: marriages that have failed and countries that have broken treaties. The coming of God into this world was meant to heal relationships. The one who was called Immanuel came to heal the most important relationship of all and to ensure that, though we may be lonely, we would never need to be alone. How? It's time for the next clue.

2. Prince of peace[2]

We live in a world where peace is a precious commodity. The history of the human race is scarred with war. War between nations, war between individuals, war between families. The world of the late twentieth century is a time when we have known an unprecedented period of relative 'peace'. But still, people have been killed in Northern

[2]Isaiah 9:6.

Ireland, the Lebanon, Vietnam, Sri Lanka, Iran, Iraq, the Falkland Islands, Ethiopia, Nicaragua, Kuwait, Saudi Arabia, Egypt and Israel, just to mention a few. Since the end of the Second World War, over twenty million people have died as a result of armed conflicts. Ours is not a peaceful society. Indeed, at the very time when we boast of our hard fought peace (a contradiction if ever there was one) we have the potential to wreak destruction on a scale never seen before. Over forty countries have nuclear power at the time of writing. One nuclear Cruise missile has the equivalent of fifteen times the explosive power of all the explosives used in the whole of the Second World War. It was J. F. Kennedy who declared, 'Unless mankind destroys war, war will destroy mankind.'

The much vaunted I.N.F. Treaty signed in December 1987 by President Reagan and Mr Gorbachev only rid the world of 4% of its nuclear armoury. We may disagree as to how peace in our time may be achieved, but that peace is much sought after is not in doubt.

The God of the whole universe is so committed to peace that he became a human baby, vulnerable, helpless and crying. He came into a world of war and peace, dirt and hurt, injustice and inequality, oppression and despair, poverty and famine. He came on the most daring rescue mission in history. He came to rescue his creation and save it. Save it? From who or what? It's time for the third and final clue.

3. Jesus[3]

The very name that the angel told Joseph to give to the child Mary was to bear, says it all. It means literally 'The Lord saves.' But what do you and I need saving from? We look

[3]Matthew 1:21.

around us at the world in which we live and we can't think what we need saving from. Everything seems so secure, at least on one level, although, as we have seen, in reality things are slightly different. In facing up to our world and how it really is, we have to face up to ourselves. If we are honest, we are not the people we would like others to think we are. Mark Twain put it very succinctly when he said, 'Everybody is a moon, and has a dark side that he never shows to anybody.'

We know our own motives, minds and thoughts – how we fail to live up to our own standards, never mind anyone else's. The Bible has a word for this which sums it up aptly: sin. At first glance it might appear a bit old-fashioned or too religious. But in reality this is how the Christian faith describes our failure to live up to our standards, other people's standards and, ultimately, God's standards. There are various expressions for this in the Old and New Testament. One of them means, very simply, to fail to come up to the standard required. It has the idea of throwing a javelin and never reaching the qualifying mark, or firing an arrow at a target and never hitting the bulls-eye. We all fail to reach the standards God sets for each of our lives. Deep down, we know we do too. It is surely the height of arrogance for anyone to assume that we can live a life good enough to reach God's standards. Somebody had to come to live a life that good, however. He came at the first Christmas.

For Mary, there was no doubt that her baby was to be very special and as she saw him grow up she must have wondered how it would all work out. Beginning with shepherds and wise men, and through his childhood, she observed that in some ways he was a child like any other, yet in another he was totally different. Perhaps it wasn't until the end of his short life that she really understood how special he was. But as time went by, she must have suspected that her child would be the one to end the loneliness for millions of people; loneliness from each other, and loneliness from God himself.

From now on, people might be lonely, but the possibility was that they might never be alone again. Her son was God-with-us.

The Old Testament was written in Hebrew and the Hebrew word for peace is 'shalom'. It is an all-embracing peace that is implied. Peace with God, peace with oneself, peace with other people and peace with the created world. The baby that came into the world one night in a side-alley of the Roman Empire was the one who is able to bring that kind of peace. Peace to a world, and to individuals, who are crying out for peace.

The whole reason for the birth of this special child was that he might live up to his name. Humanity was, and is still, in need of a saviour. Sooner or later, we have to face up to the truth of ourselves. The poet T. S. Eliot astutely observed in the *Four Quartets* that, 'Human kind/Cannot bear very much reality.' The truth about our lives may be uncomfortable to bear, but it must be faced. We are not all we think we are. We need saving from ourselves, and from each other. Walter Lippman, a self-confessed atheist, put his finger on it shortly after the Second World War: 'We ourselves were so sure that at long last the generation had arisen, keen and eager to put this disorderly world aright and fit to do it. We meant so well and tried so hard, and look what we have made of it. We can only muddle from muddle to muddle. What is required is a new kind of man.'

So, who is this 'new kind of man'? What is he like? What did he say? What did he do? How did people react to him? Did they make the connection between how they felt and lived, and the things that he said and did? Do you?

25

For further reading

Reclaiming Friendship, Ajith Fernando (IVP, 1991).
What's the Point of Christmas? J. John (Lion, 1988).
Luke 1:26 – 2:52.

3

The way to live

In 1980, the Trade Union leader Jimmy Reid announced that he was leaving the Communist Party. He was interviewed on television as to why he had taken this decision. Towards the end of the interview, he was asked if, having left the Communist Party, he now believed in God. He grinned, thought for a while and replied, 'I don't know about that, but if there is a God, then I hope he's like Jesus.'

A small girl was drawing on a piece of paper. Her mother was curious as to what her daughter was doing. So she asked, 'What are you drawing, Susan?' 'I'm drawing a picture of Jesus', she replied. 'But no-one knows what Jesus looked like!' The little girl turned in triumph, 'They will when I've finished drawing this!'

One of the basic questions in life is, if there is a God, what is he like? Can we indeed know? Jerry Lewis, the American comedian, once said, 'There are three things that are real. God, human folly and laughter. Since the first two are beyond our comprehension, we must do what we can with the third.' A pretty depressing summary!

Somebody else who found God hard to understand was

the poet, author and playwright Samuel Beckett. He made his plays even harder to understand by writing some of them in French, despite the fact that he was Irish! In his play 'Waiting for Godot', he has the principal characters, two tramps called Vladimir and Estragon, waiting for a character called Godot. They wait, wait and keep on waiting. The plot is not exactly fast-moving. The play ends with them still waiting! Mike Starkey has written a poem suggesting what might happen if Godot were actually to appear on stage.

The audience were all well dressed
and sat contentedly depressed
by the pointlessness of the modern age
when suddenly Godot walked on stage.

The jawbones of the actors dropped
when suddenly their waiting stopped.
The prompt girl tried to find the page
where Godot's meant to walk on stage.

The usherette could sense disaster
when the manager ran past her
working out the extra wage
now that Godot had walked on stage.

The critics said they found it hard
to take such joy in avant garde
it spoilt the spirit of the age
to witness Godot walk on stage.

The audience agreed that it would it wreck it
to have a happy end in Beckett
and so they all walked out in rage
when they saw Godot walk on stage.

But a lady in a crocheted shawl
sitting in the lower stalls
leaned and whispered to her friend
that she DID like plays with a happy end.[1]

Christianity says, as it were, that Godot (or God) *has* walked onto the stage of this planet. In the person of Jesus of Nazareth, he came into our world and showed us what God really is like, and what it is to be fully human. He experienced what it was like to be born (and what is more human than that?), to live as a poor carpenter, and eventually experienced what it was like to die. He identified fully with the human race. He treated the unrespectable with respect and treated everyone as individuals of worth. He never talked to two people in the same way, but always showed a love and concern for people as individuals.

That such a person as Jesus actually existed is not worth arguing about. There is more evidence to show that he lived than perhaps anyone else in history. Historians from non-Christian traditions, and with nothing to gain, assert that such a person did exist. From the first, second and third centuries AD Josephus, Suetonius, Tacitus and Pliny all agree that he was a real person.

What is under question is who exactly was he? He has always prompted questions. H. G. Wells the writer said, 'I am an historian, I am not a believer, but this penniless preacher from Galilee is irresistibly the centre of history.'

Various theories have been put forward about who Jesus was. A teacher, a prophet, a revolutionary, a poet and a liar. Many people from Gandhi to Dostoevsky have admired Jesus, but have rejected one important piece of information. Who did Jesus say he was?

---

[1]'Godot: in response to Samuel Beckett's play' by Mike Starkey, taken from *Frogs and Princes* (MARC Europe, 1987). Used with permission.

In one of the most outrageous statements ever made, Jesus actually claimed to be God. In the fourth historical account of the life of Jesus, the Gospel of John, he says, 'Anyone who has seen me has seen the Father' (John 14:9). Speaking in his Jewish context, it was a remark that prompted some to accuse him of blasphemy. Now this is not consistent with someone who is widely regarded as a good religious teacher. People who claim to be God these days are taken and locked up in nice rooms with soft, padded walls so they don't hurt themselves or anyone else. It is illogical to say that Jesus was a good, moral teacher. Teachers of good morals do not claim to be God!

C. S. Lewis, Oxford academic and author of the Narnia stories, described himself as perhaps the most reluctant convert to Christianity in all of England. In his book *Mere Christianity* he summed up the question of who Jesus is thus:

> A man who is merely a man and said the sort of things Jesus said would not be a good moral teacher. He would either be a lunatic – on the level of a man who claimed to be a poached egg – or else he would be the devil of hell, or something worse. You must make your choice. Either the man was, and is, the Son of God or else he is a madman.[2]

Some people who met Jesus thought he was just a good teacher. The Gospel of Mark, chapter 10, records an incident of just such a person. We don't know much about him, except that he was rich, young and enjoyed some influence in society, either as a local administrator or as a result of his wealth. He certainly wasn't shy as he asked

[2]*Mere Christianity*, C. S. Lewis (Fontana, 1970).

Jesus a very personal question in front of what would have been a fairly large crowd. He suddenly dropped on to his knees in front of Jesus and, addressing him as 'good teacher', asked him how he might obtain eternal life. Jesus' reply begins to put the young man in his rightful place. 'Why do you call me good? No-one is good – except God.' Do you see what Jesus is saying?

If we call Jesus good, and no-one is really good except God, then to call Jesus good, is to call him God! It probably wasn't what the young man wanted to hear. He had come simply to ask how he might have eternal life. Alec McCowen is an actor who has devised a one man show based on Mark's Gospel. In his book, *Personal Mark*, he observes.

> The young man, recklessly, publicly, unself-consciously, expected a formula for eternal life – as if eternal life was the equivalent of becoming a doctor, a high ranking Army officer, the top of the form; as if eternal life was the equivalent of winning an award, a prize or a diploma. Did the naiveté of the request and the humour of the situation appeal to Jesus? [3]

We can guess that it probably did. The young man tries to assure Jesus that he has passed the test – he's kept all the commandments! Jesus' response is probably to smile to himself. Here again is the arrogance of a person who thinks their life is good enough for God. But there is no reproach from Jesus. Rather, Mark tells us that Jesus looked at him and loved him. A mixture of pity and compassion? We don't know, but we do know that Jesus now stops playing the young man's game.

If the young man is serious, he must do something very

[3]*Personal Mark*, Alec McCowen (Fount, 1985).

difficult. 'Sell everything you have and give to the poor, and you will have treasure in heaven. Then come, follow me' (Mark 10:21). A bit stiff?

Some people think that Christianity is a crutch, a soft option for those people who can't cope. The media image of church helps to reinforce that view. Church is for old ladies, Thora Hird and Harry Secombe; vicars are weak, spineless individuals who could profit from several months with a bullworker and several years doing a 'proper' job; and even in the infamous soaps, Christianity has been portrayed by characters like Dot in *EastEnders* or Harold in *Neighbours*. Hardly flattering, I think you'll agree.

The Christianity of the gospels is an entirely different matter altogether. Jesus always called people to follow him in a whole hearted way, and there was always a cost. For this young man, it was the thing most precious to him – his money and possessions. For other people, it was different things. But one thing was certain. You couldn't follow Jesus of Nazareth and stay the same!

The same has been true throughout history. Countless thousands of men and women have died or been imprisoned for their faith in Jesus. A German Christian, Dietrich Bonhoeffer, who was to die in a Nazi concentration camp, summed it up: 'When Christ calls a man, he bids him come and die.'

To become a Christian is no soft option. If you want an easy life, you might as well put this book down now.

The young man had a choice. What was to dictate his life from now on? His money and possessions or the claims of Jesus? The yuppie phenomenon is not new. This young man was a yuppie, AD 30 version. Christianity speaks as much to the rich as to the poor.

Jesus never said that money was wrong, but that the *love* of money was the root of all kinds of evil (Paul recounts this in 1 Timothy 6:10). It certainly does not guarantee you happiness, despite Spike Milligan's claim that, 'Money can't buy you friends but you can get a better class of enemy.' Perhaps no one person's life has summed this up better than the life of Paul Getty III. Despite being one of the richest men in the world, his family was never free from feuding. His sons never felt that he loved them or that he had time for them. His biography described his lifestory as being of 'a wealth that afforded him no joy through five marriages, five divorces, two miserable deaths and unforgiving, unrelenting miserliness. A legend of luxury, lust and loneliness.'

The pointlessness of the pursuit of wealth was summed up for me by this story in the *Los Angeles Times*, 10th June 1983.

Dennis Barnhart was the President of an aggressive, rapidly expanding company, Eagle Computer International. From a small beginning, the firm grew rapidly and went public. As a result of this first public stock offering, the 44 year old man become a multimillionaire overnight. Then for some reason, driving his red Ferrari only blocks from the Company Headquarters, he drove 20 feet into a ravine and died.

Until 4.30 p.m., Wednesday had been the best day for Barnhart and the thriving young company, which makes small business and personal computers. Eagle had netted $37 million from the initial offering of 2.75 million shares. The stock which hit the market at $13 a share, rose as high as $27 before closing at a bid price of $15.50. That made Barnhart's ownership of 592,000 shares worth more than $9 million.

He died the same afternoon.

The young man, who had come to Jesus for an easy answer, left with the whole of his life questioned and in doubt. Faced with the man who is God, change had to occur if he was to follow Jesus. The same is true for you and me. Don't worry, he doesn't want to change everything at once! But the choice is there all the same. Who do you think Jesus is? A good teacher or the Son of God who can tell you how to run your life? The choice is yours, but as we will see later, he earned the right to tell us how to live by showing us the extent of his commitment to us. If you think he is more than a good teacher, then your life has to change.

We don't know what the response of the young man was. But throughout the history of Christianity there have been people whose attitude towards wealth and money has been radically altered by them becoming Christians. In the eighteenth century the travelling preacher and hymn writer John Wesley (best known for founding the Methodist church) restricted himself to an allowance of £30 a year despite sometimes earning up to £1,400 a year from the publication of his books. He gave the rest away to charity.

During the twentieth century there has been the example of Sir John Laing, the construction engineer and entrepreneur. During the course of his lifetime he was a multimillionaire but when he died, he left just £317 in his will. He had given the rest away.

Two people out of millions who have made the connection between the man called Jesus and their everyday life. Yes, he was a good religious teacher but he was so much more than that.

Colonel James Irwin, one of the first astronauts to walk on the moon's surface is in no doubt. 'The greatest miracle is not that man stood on the moon. It is that God came and stood on the earth.'

4

The way to choose

As human beings, the one thing we all crave for is love. More songs have been written, more poems penned and more pain caused by this, the strongest of our emotions. Which one of us hasn't sniffed a tear through a 'weepie' at the cinema, while maintaining that we had something in our eye all the time?!

Some of us have a romantic idea of love. Others are more cynical and reserved. But who hasn't felt that tinge of disappointment on February the 14th as the postman walks *past* our door, or the little flutter as *that* person walks into a room? Physically, psychologically and emotionally, we are built to give and receive love. Some people trade on this.

In most newspapers and magazines, there are adverts for various agencies that promise to solve our relationship difficulties. One of these, Dateline, is particularly successful, or at least it claims to be!

Life is empty without that someone special with whom you want to share your life. Andrew felt Jackie was a girl he could settle down with after six weeks. 'I know I'm young,' said Jackie, 'but Andrew is the one and I don't want to lose him.' Tony and Cindy said of Dateline, 'It may sound unromantic but it is logical, and it works! At least you know that the people you meet are in the market for a relationship – and that you have things in common.'

For Cindy and Tony, joining Dateline was the recipe for love – the lasting kind.

Whether you agree with Dateline or not, and you may wish to put the book down at this point while you recover, the fact that it has been so successful does raise some interesting points!

Anything goes . . .

Love is undoubtedly being sought after, more and more. But is our society equipped to deal with it? The 1960s and 1970s saw a rejection of 'traditional' values with regard to sex and love. Jane Fonda summed up the view of an entire generation when she said, 'God, for two people to live together for the rest of their lives is almost unnatural.' With a freer attitude towards sex, came an increased cynicism towards marriage and love and a focus on the sexual act itself. Malcolm Muggeridge observed, 'The orgasm has replaced the Cross as the focus of longing and the image of fulfilment.'

The yearning for love, however, has continued and grown, especially as the society in which we live has become more depersonalized and relationless. The psychologist Gunter Schmidt has written,

> Sexuality has acquired more and more of a compensatory function. It is supposed to hold mar-

riages and relationships together ... sexuality is supposed to promote self-realisation and self-esteem in a society which makes it more and more difficult to feel worth something and needed as an individual, it's supposed to drive out coldness and powerlessness in a world bureaucratised by administration, a world walled up in concrete landscapes and a world of disrupted relationships at home and in the community.[1]

And yet, in a society supposedly becoming more and more sexually aware and mature, ignorance and misunderstanding continue to prevail. The *Guardian* newspaper carried an article on the 8th of May, 1986, which showed how little people understand.

A survey was conducted in the north of England of 1,000 girls aged between fifteen and seventeen who had had some sexual experience. In all, 663 had used no contraception the first time they had sex. Of those, 437 had become pregnant resulting in 220 abortion 'patients' and 217 young mothers. Our society puts on a front of sophistication and knowledge. In reality many people are immature and ignorant. As one of the girls interviewed said, 'When you're 15, you hardly see any 15 year olds pregnant. You think, it never happens does it, it'll be alright.' Another boy added, 'I mean if she doesn't say anything then it's obvious you already think she's on the pill ... If you do it and she doesn't say anything, and gets pregnant then I class it as her own fault, and if she took me to court then I'd say that.'

In a survey carried out in 1990 by *Just 17* magazine, a staggering 70% of the fifteen-year-old boys questioned thought that a girl couldn't get pregnant if you had sex

[1]*Human Sexuality and Its Problems*, J. Bancroft (Churchill Livingstone, 1987). Used with permission.

standing up! An interesting approach to contraception but hardly a realistic one. This in a nation where a Government survey in 1991 estimated the average age at which girls had sex for the first time at thirteen and a half.

As sex and love became more and more divorced, so the dissatisfaction with love and relationships has increased too. The Merseyside poet Roger McGough wrote for many in the 1960s.

> Wasn't a bad party really
> Except for the people
> People always spoil things
> Room's in a mess
> And this one's left her clothes all over the place
> Scattered like seeds
> In too much of a hurry, that's her trouble
> Aren't we all?
>
> Think she's asleep now
> It makes you sleep
> Better than Horlicks
> Not so pretty really when you get close-up
> Wonder what her name is?
> Now she's taken all the blankets
> Too selfish that's her trouble
> Aren't we all?[2]

As the dissatisfaction with sex has grown, so has the distrust in relationships. We have already seen how the divorce figures have soared. The attitude of Morris L. Ernst sums up how many people feel: 'A sound marriage is not

[2]'Aren't We All?', Roger McGough, from *The Mersey Sound* (Penguin Books, 1967). Reprinted by permission of the Peters Fraser & Dunlop Group Ltd.

based on complete frankness; it is based on sensible reticence.'

People have become less and less tolerant of each other, although few have reached the level of Woody Allen. 'Basically my wife was immature. I'd be at home in the bath and she'd come in and sink my boats.'

So what does Christianity have to say to a society so confused, and yet apparently so sophisticated, with regard to love and sex? A society which has shown itself patently inept at conducting relationships, and in educating the young about sex. (When the Government began the campaign to warn people about the dangers of HIV and AIDS, it encountered opposition and disbelief from some teenagers who believed the whole thing was a plot to stop them having the fun their parents had enjoyed during the 60s.)

Love . . . and forgiveness

A common feeling in our society is the need for love and forgiveness, perhaps our strongest emotions. We see the results of the lack of both around us all the time. Marriages are torn apart, bosses and workers fail to communicate and countries refuse to trust each other. Yet, where one or the other is brought to bear, the results are marked and startling. Following the IRA bombing of Victoria station in February 1991 it was remarkable to hear the widow of the man killed saying that she forgave the bombers.

Who can ever forget the moving words of Gordon Wilson, the father of Marie Wilson (the nurse killed in the Enniskillen bombing in Northern Ireland on the 8th of November, 1987)? The full story has been told in the book he has written called simply *Marie*. On the day after the bombing, Gordon Wilson gave a radio interview in which he described the last minutes of his daughter's life and his feelings.

The wall collapsed . . . and we were thrown forward . . . rubble and stones . . . all around us and under us. I remember thinking . . . 'I'm not hurt' . . . but there's a pain in my shoulder . . . I shouted to Marie, 'Are you alright?' and she said, 'Yes' . . . three or four times I asked her . . . I asked her the fifth time 'Are you alright, Marie?' . . . She said, 'Daddy, I love you very much . . .' Those were the last words she spoke to me . . . I kept shouting, 'Marie, are you alright?' . . . There was no reply . . .

I have lost my daughter, but I bear no ill will, I bear no grudge. Dirty sort of talk is not going to bring her back to life . . . I don't have an answer . . . But I know there has to be a plan. If I didn't think that, I would commit suicide . . . It's part of a greater plan, and God is good . . . And we shall meet again.

The power of forgiveness was so strong that many listening to the news on car radios were forced to pull in to the side of the road as his words floated over the airways. As a Christian, he knew what it was to be forgiven and, hard though it was, could therefore forgive the people responsible for the tragedy. He wrote later,

My words were not intended as a statement of theology or of righteousness, rather they were from the heart, and they expressed exactly how I felt at the time, and as I still do. Countless sermons have been preached on the subject of forgiveness and many sermons written. I do not pretend to understand all of them . . . I prefer my conception of the simple, uncomplicated, and yet so demanding words of Christ in the Lord's Prayer.[3]

[3]*Marie: Story from Enniskillen*, Gordon Wilson and Alf McCreary (Marshall Pickering, 1990). Used with permission.

Christianity is based on a relationship of love and for-giveness. It is not based on rules or regulations, do's and don't's. Jesus always accepts people and offers them for-giveness. Yes, he does want to change us, as we mentioned at the end of the previous chapter, but first comes an acceptance that we can never experience from anyone else. Nothing we've ever done or said is too bad or too shocking for Jesus to forgive. We find an incident that shows the accepting nature of Jesus in John's account of the life of Jesus.

Love . . . for a young woman

We read in the eighth chapter that Jesus went to the Mount of Olives. From other references, it is clear that he had gone to be alone with God. Jesus' unique relationship with his father is a feature of his life on earth. From it he was able always to know the will of God, and know his power and purposes. He also knew a peace and composure that few have ever experienced.

Having spent some time in prayer, Jesus went to the temple courts in Jerusalem. As soon as people saw him, they began to gather around him. There was something about the person and character of Jesus that attracted people all the time. They might not always agree with him, but they wanted to hear what he had to say. Elsewhere, we read of whole towns coming out to hear his teachings, and they are amazed at his authority.

Suddenly, there was a stir in the crowd. Some men pushed a young woman forward. Who were they? Who was she? They were Pharisees and teachers of the Jewish Law. A sincere, proud and devoutly religious minority, they were the people who knew the Old Testament inside out. They knew what you could do, what you couldn't do, when you could do it, when you couldn't and who you couldn't do it

41

with. Theirs was indeed a religion based on rules and regulations. In fact they spent most of their time discussing the rules and regulations, and devising new interpretations.

The young woman? Well, not much is known about her apart from a few facts. She was engaged and had been found in the bed of another man. At least that tells us a bit more about the Pharisees – what kind of mentality is it that looks to find people committing adultery and catch them in the act? Imagine her feelings? Guilt? Shame? Anger? She was probably wondering what her fiancé was going to say. Her parents? His parents? And now she was brought in front of this crowd and this stranger, a carpenter's son from Nazareth, was to be her judge. Who was he? What was he going to say? And why, oh why, did she go with that guy?

Love . . . in the face of religion

The Pharisees began by asking Jesus a question. 'Teacher, this woman was caught in the act of adultery. In the Law Moses commanded us to stone such women. Now what do you say?' What they were doing was laying a trap for Jesus. Either way they thought they had him. If he were to say 'No, she shouldn't be stoned' he would be seen to be contradicting the Old Testament. If he were to say 'Yes, she should be stoned', he would be in trouble with the Roman authorities as they alone had the right to execute people, or not. Either way they'd got him, or at least they thought so.

Faced with this situation, I wonder what you or I would have done? Stalled perhaps, or tried to bluff our way through? Maybe. The one thing I don't think any of us would have done was to have bent down and started to write in the sand. However, this is exactly what Jesus did! That composure I mentioned earlier is evident here. What was he doing, drawing in the sand? Well, he could have been thinking, or stalling, or teasing them. Somebody has speculated that he drew all the things that he knew the Pharisees were guilty of, while others have wondered if he wrote down ways in which we all fail to live up to God's expectations: adultery, tax fraud, gossip, lying, dishonesty, hatred, anger, violence, bitterness, incest, lust and others. They kept on asking him what they should do, he kept on drawing.

Eventually, he straightened up. Can you imagine the suspense in the crowd? What would he say? How would they react? Jesus' reply was devastatingly simple, and simply devastating. 'If any one of you is without sin', he said, 'Let him be the first to throw a stone at her.'

'At this, those who heard began to go away one at a time, the older ones first.' I think it is significant that it was the older people in the crowd who dropped their stones first and began to move away. They realized the depth of what Jesus had just said. They realized that Jesus had gone beyond the rules and regulations to the very heart of the matter. As someone once said, 'When Jesus diagnoses you, he diagnoses you at a level deeper than you have ever known. He gets under your skin and sees the issues as they really are.'

As the implications of Jesus' words sank in, more and more people drifted away. Not one of them had lived a perfect life. They had all fallen short and been found wanting. All had 'sinned' as we defined it in the second chapter. Soon there remained simply the woman, Jesus and a pile of stones.

We now see the amazing acceptance that Jesus offers. He looked up and asked the woman, 'Woman, where are they? Has no-one condemned you?' She replied, 'No-one, sir.' 'Then neither do I condemn you. Go now and leave your life of sin.'

It is not an easy acceptance however. Jesus knew that someone would have to be punished for the woman's act of adultery. Somebody would be taken and condemned by a crowd for her unfaithfulness to her fiancé. Just as someone would have to pay the price for the failures of the Pharisees and the crowd that was so eager to stone her. That person would be Jesus himself. He it was who was to be rejected that she, and we, might know real acceptance.

The young woman encountered that acceptance and it saved her life. We don't know if she continued to follow Jesus but it is hard to imagine her abandoning the man who had given her a fresh chance. She probably made the connection with Jesus and her life.

For further reading

Marie: Story from Enniskillen, Gordon Wilson and Alf McCreary (Marshall Pickering, 1990).
John 8:1–11.

5

Dying made sense

The ultimate statistic

In her book, *Castaway*, the author Lucy Irvine describes how she replied to an advertisement in a newspaper to become 'Girl Friday' on a desert island with a man she had never met before. They undergo a marriage of convenience and arrive on the island as husband and wife. Thereafter, the island paradise becomes anything but. Things go from bad to worse as their relationship deteriorates, and reach a climax as they both face serious illness. She concludes,

> So many things did not matter any more, now that supporting what life was left in our bodies had become the only value. Sex had become irrelevant. Crudity of language had no meaning that could be offensive. My accent did not grate on George any more. Physical and intellectual powers became immaterial, and the consciousness of class, which had given rise to a few jibes between us, had disappeared. Our differences

diminished as our mutual needs increased. We were companions in want.[1]

Faced with the prospect of dying, so many things that had been important became irrelevant. Death is the great leveller. We all have to face up to it, sooner or later. Anything that we've achieved in this life we have to leave behind. There are no pockets in a shroud. We find this uncomfortable and disturbing. In many parts of society death has become the great unmentionable. It has replaced sex and politics as *the* subject to be avoided in polite conversation. We go to extraordinary lengths to avoid mentioning the word itself, preferring to employ euphemisms such as 'passed away', 'fallen asleep' and even 'snuffed it'! Strangely, we go to great pains to show who we are, even in death. An obituary or headstone that distinguishes us is important. Jim Thornton in his book, *Public Need and Private Greed*, observed, 'What man really fears is not so much extinction, but extinction with insignificance.' Death is 'the ultimate statistic', according to George Bernard Shaw: 'Ten out of ten die.'

For all our society's advances, death still remains a mystery. Tom Stoppard summed up many people's feelings on the subject in the play *Rosencrantz and Guildenstern are dead*. 'Death is not anything . . . death is not. It's the absence of presence, nothing more . . . the endless time of never coming back. A gap you can't see, and when the wind blows through it, it makes no sound.'

Death is the big unknown – the ultimate black hole. As someone remarked, 'Death, that must be hard to preach on. I mean, not many of us have had much experience of it.'

So how do we react to death? How should we react to it? What does Christianity have to say on this, perhaps the most important subject for humanity?

[1] *Castaway*, Lucy Irvine (Penguin Books, 1984).

Death . . . the end?

It was Ernest Hemingway who said, 'Life is just a dirty trick. A short trip from nothingness to nothingness.' But is death the end? For many people, not all Christians by any means, such a thought is too depressing to contemplate. H. G. Wells wrote, 'If there is no afterlife, then life is just a huge sick joke, braying across the centuries.'

We are curious about death. Mediums like Doris Stokes and Betty Shine command popularity as we seek to find out the truth. Above all we are afraid of death. Woody Allen may have been joking but he spoke for many of us. He said, 'It's not that I'm afraid of dying, I just don't want to be there when it happens.' So, what does Christianity have to say to this, the most human of all subjects?

The claim of Christianity is that death has been defeated. Not that death does not affect Christians. They do still die! But, unlike any other religion, it claims its founder died, and then came back to life. The claim is either true, or the biggest lie ever told. We'll look at the basis for this claim later on, but its effects have been seen throughout history.

Following the death of George VI, Sir Winston Churchill spoke these words in a radio broadcast:

> During the last few months, the King has walked with death as if it were a companion, an acquaintance whom he recognised and did not fear. During the last few months the King has been sustained, not only by his natural buoyancy of spirit, but also by the sincerity of his Christian faith.

One of the most famous statements of Jesus is the one said in countless funeral services every day, all over the world. It comes in the eleventh chapter of John's Gospel.

Faced with the death of a close friend, Jesus stated, 'I am the resurrection and the life. He who believes in me will live, even though he dies; and whoever lives and believes in me will never die' (verses 25–26). This was either the statement of someone delirious with grief or the most remarkable words ever spoken. Which is it? What was the context? Let's see.

A death in the family

Martha and Mary were two sisters. They were friends of Jesus, and their brother, Lazarus, is described as 'the one you love'. They were close friends. Lazarus, however, fell ill and his sisters sent word to Jesus. His reaction when he heard this news was slightly odd. He declared, 'This sickness will not end in death. No, it is for God's glory so that God's Son may be glorified through it.' Surely a very odd thing to say! Even more strange is the fact that Jesus stayed where he was. He didn't go to see Lazarus immediately.

The disciples must have been very puzzled. What was Jesus doing? Then, when two days had gone by, Jesus announced, 'Let us go back to Judea.' Now the disciples were even more worried. They'd nearly been killed in Judea! Why were they going back there now? Jesus told them that Lazarus had fallen asleep and he was going to wake him up. The disciples were even more puzzled. If he was going to wake up, why did they need to risk death by going to him? Jesus had to spell it out to his disciples. He told them Lazarus had died. Even then they didn't really understand. Thomas, one of the disciples, who has become infamous as 'the Doubter', suggested, 'Let us also go, that we may die with him.' This statement can either be seen as one of the bravest declarations of loyalty, or as a pessimistic pronouncement of doom. After all, Thomas is often portrayed as being a real 'doom and gloom merchant', always looking on the grim side of life.

However, Jesus did travel to Bethany to see his friends. When he arrived, Martha, who was the more practical of the two sisters, went out to meet him. She recognized that if Jesus had been there, her brother might not have died. Jesus reminded her that her brother would rise again. Being a good Jew, she gave the right religious answer. 'I know he will rise again in the resurrection at the last day.' It was then that Jesus made that remarkable claim to be the resurrection and the life. He asked Martha if she believed this. Her religious answers are no longer good enough. She had to come to realize who Jesus is. She did believe.

After speaking to Mary, and having to answer the same question, Jesus moved to the tomb. This would have been in the side of a hill, possibly a cave of some sort. He asked that the grave be opened. Martha, ever practical, pointed out that there would be a strong smell because the body would have begun to decompose. Jesus rebuked her mildly for her disbelief. This was not the time to be guided by what was sensible or even rational. This was to be extraordinary.

Then Jesus prayed. We don't have too many incidents of Jesus' prayers being recorded. When we are allowed to eavesdrop, however, it is very revealing. There is an intimacy that is very rare. He calls God 'Father'. In fact the word that Jesus uses is 'Abba', the Hebrew word for 'Daddy'. As God's Son, there is even so a dependence on the Father.

There is also, however, an authority. Having prayed, Jesus turned to the tomb and with all the power of the Son of God, shouted, 'Lazarus, come out!' (The authority of Jesus was a feature of his life. Early on, the people remarked that his teaching had authority, unlike that of their own teachers.)

Here, his authority boomed into the great unknown. Even death had to bow to this power. The watching crowd must have gasped as they suddenly saw a figure emerging from the grave. Struggling to walk, wrapped in eight feet of cloth and embalmed in seventy pounds of spices, the greatest of Jesus' miracles walked back from the dead. Hollywood would be hard pressed to match it! Even at this dramatic demonstration of the supernatural, Jesus was still practical. 'Take off the grave clothes and let him go.' Christianity is literally a down-to-earth religion.

Blind faith?

But is the Christian belief that death has been defeated simply based on this incident? No, it most certainly isn't. This is not the only story recorded in the gospels of death being beaten. The most important is the resurrection of Jesus himself.

Jesus' resurrection is so important that the Apostle Paul, writing to one of the first churches at Corinth, said that if there is no resurrection of the dead, then there is no Christianity. If the resurrection of Jesus can be disproved, then the whole of Christianity is a waste of time.[1] So, what is the evidence for this extraordinary claim?

Exhibit a, b, c, . . .

a. The change in the lives of the disciples

Following the death of Jesus, which we'll look at in detail in chapter 8, his followers became dispirited and scared. Some deserted the cause very quickly, while others retreated into the background. They were frightened, disillusioned and ready to return home. Yet suddenly, they became a daring, bold, courageous and purposeful unit which was to change the world beyond recognition. Many died cruel and painful deaths – martyrs to a cause they fervently believed in.

[1]Read 1 Corinthians 15.

Would they really have been prepared to die for something they knew to be false?

The church is growing today at a rate faster than at any other time in its history. In China, when the western missionaries were removed following the Communist takeover in 1949, the church numbered one million. When the Bamboo Curtain lifted in 1984, conservative estimates put the church at forty million! The group of men and women who gathered in Jerusalem after the death of a carpenter from Nazareth were the founders of a movement that is still affecting the lives of more people than anything else. Is it really based on a lie?

b. The lack of a body
The easiest way for the Roman and Jewish authorities to have quashed the beginnings of Christianity would have been for them to have produced the corpse of Jesus. As soon as they heard the first Christians claiming that Jesus had risen from the dead, the production of the dead body of the itinerant teacher from Nazareth would have meant that the claim was short lived. In Palestine at the time, it was not unusual for small religious groups and sects, whose leader had been executed, to claim that he had risen from the dead. But the resurrection of Jesus took place in unusual circumstances. The tomb had been guarded by soldiers after it was sealed. Yet no body was produced. It couldn't be as there was no corpse to be found.

c. The down-to-earth nature of the disciples
The followers of Jesus were ordinary people. They were fishermen, tax collectors and housewives. Even given the rash nature of the inhabitants of the Galilean region, they did not expect Jesus to rise again from the dead. That is clear from their reactions to the appearances of Jesus. This discounts one theory – that they were hallucinating. Firstly,

51

to hallucinate something, you have to expect to see it. Secondly, it is unheard of in medical science for five hundred people to have the same hallucination at the same time. Yet that is what the Apostle Paul claims to have happened as, in writing to the church at Corinth, he describes how Jesus appeared to Simon Peter, the other disciples and, at one stage, five hundred people.[2]

Alternative theories . . .

Some people have tried to see how the resurrection of Jesus can be explained away or discounted altogether. There are two main theories:

a. The wrong tomb theory
This theory puts forward the idea that, overcome with grief, the women went to the wrong tomb on that Easter morning. They met a gardener who told them, 'He is not here', meaning that they had come to the wrong place in the graveyard. They had gone to the wrong tomb, disorientated by their grief, ragged emotions and the early half-light of dawn. Is this credible? The women were there at the burial of Jesus. They would have remembered the spot alright. Can you imagine forgetting where a close friend or relative is buried?

Also, the man that the women met that morning did say something else. He uttered the words that have greeted Christians every Easter morning since: 'He is risen!'

b. The swoon theory
This is perhaps the one that requires more faith than Christianity itself. It suggests that Jesus did not die on the cross, he merely fainted. As he lay in the tomb, the cool air revived him.

[2] 1 Corinthians 15:4–6.

He recovered consciousness, unwrapped the eight feet of bandages which his body was covered in, moved a stone at the door of the tomb (which could only be opened from the outside), overcame a squad of fifty Roman soldiers (whose punishment for failure to guard a dead Jesus would have been their own deaths), shrugged off a wound in his side and the effects of the beatings the Romans had inflicted upon him, and walked unnoticed across the city of Jerusalem that was packed with pilgrims from all over the Middle East for one of the major religious festivals. He then appeared to his disciples in such a way that they thought he had risen from the dead! His back was probably broken, but he made Rambo appear like a picnic for Sylvester Stallone. As I said, it requires a lot of believing!

There is, however, a simple way of destroying the basis of such a proposal. The gospel writers tell us that when the soldier pushed the spear into the side of Jesus, blood and water came out. Doctors today know what that means. A watery serum, accompanied by semi-solid dark red clots of blood, is a recognized test for certifying a patient dead. They did not know that when the gospels were written. Jesus was definitely dead.

To sum up

There is more evidence and many books have been written on the subject of the resurrection. See the details at the end of the chapter for more information. The resurrection is the most important part of the Christian faith. If it is not true, then the whole Christian message can be disproved, so it is worth making sure. One person who is convinced is Sir Edward Clarke, a former High Court Judge. He has written,

> As a lawyer, I have made a prolonged study of the evidence for the events of Easter Day. To me, the

evidence is conclusive, and over and over again, in the High Court, I have secured the verdict on evidence not so compelling. As a lawyer I accept the Gospel evidence unreservedly as the testimony of truthful men to facts that they were able to substantiate.[3]

The resurrection of Jesus is more than a symbol of what can happen in an individual's life or in society in general. It is a historical event that changed the nature of life and death for ever. Its claims are well documented and though countless attempts have been made to disprove or discredit it, it has stood the tests of time and examination. It means that death need not be feared, although quite naturally humanity will fear the process of dying. Death need not be the taboo subject that it has become in some parts of the world today, noticeably in the West.

It does not invalidate grief or sadness. Jesus himself wept at the death of his friend Lazarus, even though he knew he would raise him to life again! But in the words of C. S. Lewis, Christians need never say goodbye – simply *au revoir*.

For more information

Dying To Live, Jim Graham (Marshall, Morgan & Scott, 1984).
Who Moved the Stone?, F. Morison (STL, 1983).
The Day Death Died, Michael Green (IVP, 1982).
Luke 24:1–49.

[3]Quoted by Michael Green in *The Day Death Died* (IVP, 1982), p. 37.

6

The dark side of the force!

Throughout the history of Hollywood, an ever popular type of film has been the horror movie. From numerous incarnations of *Dracula, Frankenstein, The Exorcist, The Omen, Nightmare on Elm Street* and *Ghostbusters* to the seemingly innocent *Teenage Mutant Hero Turtles*, the struggle of good against evil has always been of interest for some, and a source of fascination for many. In some films this is portrayed in graphic and gory detail while in others, such as *The Silence of the Lambs* it takes the form of a psychological thriller. The battle between good and evil is behind most fairy tales and pantomimes. The interest in this battle takes many forms. Mike Gatting, the former England cricket captain, spoke for many when he declared, 'I believe in a bit of everything – God, the supernatural, ghosts, superstitions, U.F.O.s ... I like to keep my options open.'

No popular breakfast television programme or daytime magazine edition is seemingly complete without an astrologer, palmist, tarot card expert, medium or clairvoyant. From Russell Grant to Patrick Walker, Stephen King to

Dennis Wheatley, the possibilities of the supernatural are fascinating, whether they be fictional or imagined.

On a recent visit to a local comprehensive school, 80% of a class of fourteen-year-olds confessed to having tried a ouija board. Four boys volunteered the fact that the night before they had played with a ouija board in the local cemetery. In the United States, it is estimated that there are some 100,000 witches, while 5,000 people are employed full-time working on astrology charts for over ten million Americans.

Even *before* she died, the popular medium Doris Stokes claimed to have talked to the late Marilyn Monroe and Elvis Presley. Meanwhile, newspapers wrote of the 'seductive charms of the occult' (*The Times*) and proclaimed magic to be 'one of the boom industries of the late twentieth century' (*The Sunday Telegraph*). Elsewhere, social workers began to approach churches for help in dealing with the victims of satanic ritual abuse. Although this caused an enormous controversy in Britain as the cases in Lancashire, Nottinghamshire and the Orkneys were reviewed (with accusations in some newspapers of scaremongering tactics by some Christian groups), there remained sufficient evidence for most people to suspect something was going on, even if not in these cases.

Despite the protestations of some church leaders and theologians, the occult is alive and well. The fascination even began to spread to science. Colin Wilson in his book on the occult noted that,

> In science, a new cycle has begun, a revolt against the old rigid reductionism, a recognition that 'materialism' leaves half the universe unexplained. Biologists, psychologists and even physicists are cautiously trying their way into new worlds. They are acknowledging at last that they are dealing with a living universe, a universe full

of strange forces. The magic of the past was an intuitive attempt to understand and control these forces; the science of the future will be a fully conscious attempt.[1]

There are many reasons for this fascination with the occult (*lit.* 'the unknown'). Some are as old as civilization itself – superstition, paganism and the natural human desire to explore the mysterious and the secret. As children we can all remember the attraction of exploring somewhere mysterious or of doing something we were expressly forbidden to do. Other reasons are new – the realization of the emptiness of materialism and the pursuit of possessions, the natural hunger for power and excitement and the failure of the church in the West to provide anything remotely lively or interesting.

This fascination has appeared in many forms. From newspaper horoscopes to serious devotees of black magic, the possibility of an evil spiritual force has been explored. Extra-sensory perception, automatic writing, charms, spiritualism, fortune telling, palmistry, tarot cards, crystals, psychometry, ouija, necromancy and clairvoyancy are just some of the variety on offer. One strange group even offered *the purple energy plate*. The saleswoman, Wendy Rose explained, 'The atomic structure of the plate is attuned with the energy of the universe. If a sick person picks up the plate, you can see the energy flooding out of the plate into the person.'

For some people, the mention of spiritual forces, ghosts, evil spirits and the Devil is hard to take seriously. 'Surely it was the primitive, pre-scientific way of looking at things? The devil is a convenient way of explaining away all the evil within each one of us. Nowadays, we have psychology,

[1] *The Occult*, Colin Wilson (Panther, 1979).

medicine and science to explain all that was referred to as the work of the devil.'

Freud estimated that the 'demonic' was the 'base and evil wishes deriving from impulses which have been rejected and repressed in one's personality', while Jung labelled it as 'autonomous complexes, the parts of our personality we have difficulty in admitting to ourselves'. So there!

This view is a common one amongst many people. In a paper on the subject, Michael Wilson, a lecturer at Birmingham University, wrote, 'I am a twentieth-century Western cultured man and I do not perceive people as if they were possessed. This is not the frame of reference in which I think . . . I see it in psychological and sociological terms.'

Yet to others, dealing with evil spirits is an everyday occurrence. One vicar in the Church of England tells of dealing with many people who have been troubled by such spirits. A visiting church leader from China roared with laughter and disbelief when he was told that most English vicars did not believe in the existence of evil spirits – to him they were commonplace.

In people affected by evil spirits, it is common to find some evidence of occult involvement, either directly or indirectly. But what are the dangers involved in exploring the occult? For some clues, we'll look at what happened when Jesus met a man who had been taken over by evil spirits. Following a stormy crossing of the Sea of Galilee, Jesus and his closest friends were met by a terrifying sight. A naked and deranged man met them on the shoreline, dragging broken chains behind him and shouting at the top of his voice. From the account we can learn several things about the man and what happens when we get involved with the occult. He was physically very strong and powerful, but he used that power to terrorize other people. It brought fear and physical danger to those he came into contact with, and brought harm to himself.

He apparently used to sit around graveyards without any clothes on. Perhaps this hinted at an obsession with death, dying or with a dead relative. He was alone, separated from his wife, children and friends.

The man Jesus met was frightened, powerful, shameless and incapable of being himself. When Jesus asked him his name, he replied 'Legion' (one translation uses the more menacing and evocative term 'mob'!). His own personality was suppressed. He did not know who he was.

He is perhaps an extreme example but, having talked with those who deal with such people today, such 'symptoms' are common amongst those who have dealt in the realm of the occult: an obsession with or fear of death; an occasional demonstration of unnatural strength; a complete lack of guilt or shame; a subduing of the person's own identity and personality; and an inability to make or maintain normal family or friendly relationships. Yet is it an extreme? All of us experience some of the symptoms, to a lesser degree or another. We'll examine three of them.

1. Who am I?

In the past decades, many people have crowded into the consulting rooms of psychologists and psychotherapists unsure as to who they really are. Identity is seemingly increasingly difficult to maintain. For all our desire and effort to impress others by the acquisition of material possessions, we are increasingly unsure of who we are. From the poor to the wealthy, a lack of identity is a common complaint – take the actor Peter Sellers, for example. Shortly before his death, he wrote the following: 'I haven't a clue who Peter Sellers is. I have no personality of my own. I reached my present position by working hard and not following Socrates' advice "Know Thyself". I couldn't follow it if I wanted to. To me, I am a complete stranger.' The man of a thousand voices, from Inspector Clouseau to the Goons, could not recognize his own. His fourth wife, Lynne Frederick, added that his mind was 'in a constant state of turmoil about what his purpose was on this planet and whether it was all worthwhile'.

For the man who met Jesus on that beach, the experience was one that restored to him his own identity and personality. After the evil spirits have been dealt with, the man is described as 'sitting at Jesus' feet, dressed and in his right mind'. It is a lovely picture of the effect an encounter with Jesus always has. The process of following Jesus is a voyage of discovering who we really are, and the people we were always meant to be. (It does not mean that everybody who is mentally ill, or has a personality disorder, is involved with the occult or needs to be delivered of evil spirits. However, together with psychological, psychiatric and medical treatments, this may be appropriate in some cases.)

2. A family reunion

The man desperately wanted to go with Jesus, but his request to do so was refused. Instead Jesus told the man to go home and tell what God had done for him. We can only speculate what the scene was like outside the man's house. The children, happily playing by their home, recognized the figure walking down the road towards them. Perhaps they shuddered as the memories of fear, anger and abuse came into their minds, recalling the last time they had seen their father. Calling to their mother, they stood transfixed as the silhouette drew closer and closer. Hearing their anxious cries, their mother ran out to them. She too was fearful as she remembered the final months before her husband went away. Imagine her surprise as she saw a very different man returning to her. This was the man that she had married.

It is not easy to be a parent or child today. The awesome

responsibility of being a father or mother weighs heavily on many people, whilst for others being a child in a world that treats them like an adult is very difficult.

A group of fourteen-year-olds were recently asked to write down the first words that came to mind when they thought of their father. The subsequent list is illuminating: tall, old, laughing, cooking, black socks, knowledgeable, awkward, authority, hate, adultery, caring, deceitful, dependable, bald, unsettled, confused, insensitive and stubborn.

When the man met Jesus, he was alone – friendless and separated from his wife and children. He returned to them a changed man, able now to maintain relationships. He wasn't perfect and he would make mistakes – we all do – but with the evil expelled, he at least had a chance to be a parent, husband and friend once more. Following Jesus offers the opportunity to restore relationships, first with God and then with people. It might not be easy and may well be painful, but it will be worth it.

3. Guilty or not?

The third symptom that the man was suffering from was the inability to feel shame or guilt. Trying to cut oneself on stones and wandering around a graveyard without any clothes on does not suggest a conscience sorely aware of conventional morality! He was a man without shame.

All of us, at times, get confused as to what is right or wrong. It might not be a big question such as 'Is there such a thing as a just war', but ethical questions arise every day. It might be whether we tell the truth or not, in a situation where it is not in our interests to do so, or something more simple at the office, college or school. We ignore those little perks at work that everyone takes for granted – the pens and paper that fall into our pockets on the way out of the office, the expense claim that isn't quite accurate because we can't remember exactly how much we paid, or more seriously, the tax return that isn't entirely honest. Whether it be a multinational corporation or the equivalent of a dispute in the playground, our sense of right or wrong depends on how much we have to gain.

One of the things that appealed to me when I was becoming a Christian was the way in which the Bible was utterly realistic in its description of humanity. The people are described 'warts and all'. The Old Testament characters such as David or Samson are portrayed as they really were – frail humans incapable of living life God's way. The disciples of Jesus are shown as being prone to the same desires for status, position and power as anyone else. This feature is admirable when describing some figure from history, but it becomes decidedly uncomfortable when it starts to get closer to home.

Perhaps you know of the parable of the good shepherd that Jesus told. Our mind focuses on the nice comforting picture of a shepherd braving death and danger to bring us home. It is indeed a warm, powerful and lively illustration of God's love for us, and the lengths he is prepared to go to in order to bring us to himself.

There is, however, an uncomfortable side to the story as well. We are, by implication, like sheep. This is not a complimentary comparison. Living in a predominantly urban society, not many of us are familiar with sheep except for meeting them at the meal table when our situation is infinitely preferable to theirs.

A conversation with any shepherd will soon tell us how unflattering the comparison is. Adjectives such as stupid, wilful, selfish, jealous and helpless would be liberally sprinkled throughout the description. However uncomfortable it is, it has to be faced up to. If we are honest, our motives are not always unselfish, generous and altruistic. We *are* like sheep.

If we are honest with ourselves, the truth can often hurt.

We are not the people we think we are, or like others to think we are. Our motives are not always pure or in the interests of others. Coming to terms with who we are as people is always difficult. As we discover more about ourselves, we are not that impressed with what we find. We want to hide from other people and ourselves. The last person we want to meet is a perfect person who knows us better than we know ourselves.

Yet again we have a choice to make – to face up to Jesus and ourselves or to ignore him and carry on pretending to ourselves and others. We can try to hide in the pursuit of power, popularity or even the fascination of the 'occult', but ultimately we have to face up to the real issues.

For the man who had been controlled by the evil spirits, he (and they) had no doubt as to who Jesus was, and to his importance. Meeting Jesus on that beach, there had been a loud cry of recognition: 'What do you want with me, Jesus, Son of the Most High God?' The result had been the restoration of that man's dignity, personality, relationships and self-respect. He went home to his family, and to himself.

For us the question is again – who do we think Jesus is, and what is our response to him going to be?

If we have been interested in or affected by the occult (either directly or indirectly) it may be that it is a barrier to us seeing who Jesus really is. If you are in that situation, don't worry, there is a way out. Go and see your church minister or leader for advice, or ask a Christian friend for advice. Jesus was able to deal with what was happening to that man, and he wants to help you too.

For more information

The Occult Web, Tom Walker (UCCF, 1987).
Hidden Warfare, David Watson (Kingsway Publications, 1987).
Paganism and the Occult, Kevin Logan (Kingsway Publications, 1988).
Read Luke 8:26–39.

7

We're all the same

Women are brave, the stronger sex, there's no doubt about that. I meet so many women who never cease to amaze me. They are definitely the better problem solvers. They sort things out and are more confident about themselves and they're much more honest about their emotions and feelings. A woman will say what she feels, a man won't. A man will be afraid of being judged and ridiculed. A woman will be quite straightforward and honest and I like that because I'm like that. But a lot of men won't tell you about their emotions, or talk about being afraid or crying or anything like that and women will. For that reason women are more real (Robert Kilroy-Silk).[1]

The oldest battle that there has ever been is the battle of the sexes. Are we really the same as each other or are we

[1] Robert Kilroy-Silk, quoted in *SHE* magazine, August 1990.

different to each other? Are men more logical than women or women more intuitive than men?

Some people obviously think so! Some American university students were asked to indicate which adjectives from a list of 300 words were typically associated with either women or men. The students were able to categorize over 90%. Women were associated with being: affectionate, appreciative, attractive, charming, gentle, dependent, submissive and talkative. Men on the other hand were seen as: adventurous, aggressive, ambitious, assertive, confident, independent, logical and stable. (Feel free to disagree!) Whether they were right or not, the interesting thing is that they felt able to categorize words in this way, and so show how we think of men and women. We think certain characteristics are 'feminine' while some remain 'masculine'. This is carried over to how we think of different jobs and who we think is suitable to do them. A group of young people were recently asked to say whether they thought the following jobs were masculine or feminine: doctor, nurse, gardener, engineer, lawyer, *au pair*, refuse collector, milk deliverer, chief constable, supermarket manager, supermarket checkout cashier. The results were fascinating and gave way to some very heated arguments! The awkwardness of the term 'milk deliverer' for example shows how we assume certain occupations as being suitable for one gender or another. This was highlighted when a Swedish man was nearly deported from the UK for being employed as an *au pair*. The Government definition of an *au pair* was a woman!

In recent years, however, the perception of women has been altered radically. Advances have been made in the roles that women play in society that were unthinkable one hundred years ago. Female Prime Ministers and Presidents have been elected, laws have been passed to ensure that gender is not an opportunity for prejudice and the traditional roles of women as simply 'wife' or 'mother' have been questioned. Between 1961 and 1981, the number of people in the work-force rose by over two million as married women returned to work or sought employment for the first time. By halfway through the 1980s, 60% of all married women in Great Britain were in paid employment of some kind or another.

The umbrella label for this movement was 'feminism', a warcry for many and a dirty word for some. The *Fontana Dictionary of Modern Thought* defines feminism as: 'The advocacy of rights and equality of women in social, economic and political spheres, a commitment to the fundamental alteration of women's role in society.'

For many people, both men and women, this is seen as a good aim. Two feminist writers, Luise Eichenbaum and Susie Orbach, summed up, in their book *What Do Women Want*, how they thought men and women should develop their thinking about each other.

> For too long we have laboured under the myth
> that men are big and strong and independent;
> that women are passive, helpless and dependent
> ... The models women have are that they should
> nurture, care and provide. As feminists we say
> 'No!' Women do not need to be dependent on
> men – they can be independent.[2]

Yet to many there is one barrier as women seek equality in society. The church itself remains a symbol of male domination, chauvinism and sexism. It is an institution traditionally organized by men for men, led by men and in which the majority of the membership are women. Many women are frustrated at the male domination of the

[2]*What Do Women Want?* L. Eichenbaum and S. Orbach (Fontana, 1984).

church and the way in which women are encouraged into certain roles, but not others. In *A Woman in Your Own Right*, a book charting the history of the Women's Movement, Anne Dickson writes that in the nineteenth century,

> [Women] filled the pews and became the standard bearers of the moral vanguard. A new female stereotype emerged – of a nature which expressed itself through moral superiority, virtue, patience, and long-suffering devotion to others. This refinement still exists today in attempts to shield women from sights too violent, words too obscene, affairs too worldly and positions too responsible![3]

The debate over the ordination of women to the priesthood of the Church of England has summed up for many people the situation facing women in the church. Yet it is only part of the picture. There are now many denominations around the world that do ordain women, including the Methodist, Baptist and United Reformed Church. Indeed if one examines the Anglican Communion as a whole (of which the Church of England is only a part), six out of sixteen provinces began to ordain women to the priesthood between 1974 and 1983. By 1990 it was estimated that there were nearly 1,500 women priests and two women bishops. Even before the historic vote in November 1992, in the Church of England there were estimated to be 1,200 women deacons (a sort of half-way stage to becoming priests), seven women canons, two rural deans and over eighty women in charge of parishes.

The campaign to ordain women as priests even attracted the support of a major advertising agency, GKN. The cost of the campaign would have been over £100,000 a year but it was given free! The campaign included posters of a woman

[3]*A Woman In Your Own Right*, Anne Dickson (Quartet Books, 1982).

leading a service and the slogan 'will our church be safe in her hands?'

The deputy chairman of GKN, Kitty Hagan explained why her company had decided to back the campaign.

> I realised that women in the Church were not loony, radical feminists. The issue was simply about their inability to get into higher management in the Church, but that they are legally constrained from moving up. Many women in business are dealing with things like male chauvinism in the boardroom, which are petty by comparison. These women cannot even get into the boardroom.

For many, the church's attitude towards women is even more shocking when one examines the attitude of its founder, Jesus, %owards the women he encountered. He livgd in a culture that relegated women to second-class citizens. One group of religious people even began each day with the prayer, 'Blessed art thou O Lord our God who hast not made me a slave, a Gentile or a woman.'

Elsewhere some Jewish men were encouraged to ignore their wife if they met her in public, whilst a wife could be divorced simply at the request of her husband! Into this culture and society came Jesus, showing a remarkable regard for women and a healthy disregard for the conventions of his day. He talked to women in public, touched them in compassion and listened to them with patience. He included them amongst his closest friends and taught them with his male disciples – a very radical move in an environment where it was forbidden to give women religious instruction. Academics are struck by the equality with which Jesus treated men and women alike. Mary Evans, in her book *Women in the Bible*, concludes that,

Jesus healed women, he allowed them to touch him and follow him; he spoke without restraint of women, to women and with women. He related to women primarily as human beings rather than sexual beings, *i.e.* he was interested in them as persons, seeing their sex as an integral part but by no means the totality of their personality.[4]

Another feminist writer, Mary Wilson-Kastner, remains firm in her admiration of Jesus' respect for the women of his time. In *Faith, Feminism and Christ* she writes:

His attentiveness to women as people was rare in the context of his culture and remarkably sensitive ... He does not proclaim a part of his gospel to women and most of it to men ... Jesus never says anything demeaning to women, trivialises them or praises their 'special contribution'. In his own presentation of himself, he compares himself to a mother hen; in describing his mission he assumes the attributes of Wisdom, the feminine personification of the divine activity; and in one of his parables he compares God to a housewife seeking a lost coin.[5]

There are numerous examples of Jesus' attitude to women in the historical accounts of his life. From the casting out of a demon from the daughter of a Syro-Phonecian woman, to Jesus healing a woman with a menstrual disorder (menorrhagia) his remarkable acceptance of women shows his willingness to break down the long held taboos of his society. Writer Mary Hayter asserts that,

[4]*Women in the Bible*, Mary Evans (Paternoster Press, 1983), p. 44.
[5]*Faith, Feminism and Christ*, Mary Wilson-Kastner (Fortress Press, 1983).

God deals with the human race, male and female, as a unity. He does not treat the male half in one way, the female half in another. Essentially the New Testament writers, following the example of Jesus himself, treat women equally. No one can read the New Testament without immediately being aware that it thrills with the sense of barriers longstanding being broken down.[6]

The instance of the healing of the woman who had been ill for years shows the extent to which Jesus was prepared to go. Both Mark and Luke record the incident, and go into graphic detail (see Mark 5:22–43 and Luke 8:41–56).

Jesus came back home to Galilee and was welcomed by a large crowd, eager to see and hear him. A man called Jairus, an important figure in the local community suddenly threw himself at Jesus' feet. Apparently his only daughter was very ill and it was feared that she was critical. Jesus agreed to accompany the man home and to see what could be done for the girl.

Both Mark and Luke tell us that something remarkable then occurred. As the crowd followed Jesus and Jairus, probably becoming increasingly excited yet not daring to say out loud the hope that the girl could be healed, Jesus stopped and asked, 'Who touched me?'

If we can imagine ourselves at Wembley for a pop concert, or in the rush hour at a railway station pressing to get on to a train, then we can begin to realize how difficult it would be to identify who touched him. This was no royal walkabout with crush barriers or security guards but a living, seething mob determined not to miss out on the latest incident in the action-packed life of Jesus of Nazareth.

His closest followers obviously saw how ridiculous the

[6]*New Eve in Christ*, Mary Hayter (S.P.C.K., 1987).

request was as they seemingly teased Jesus, pointing out the squeeze around him and of which he was the cause. But it seems he had sensed someone touch him in a special way and kept on asking, 'Who touched me?'

Eventually, a woman stepped forward. It later became apparent that she had come a long way, perhaps as far as thirty miles on foot. She had been ill for twelve long years and her whole life had been altered by her illness. Her disease was both embarrassing and socially unacceptable, rendering her ritually unclean and unable to take a normal role in everyday life. Today it can be treated by a relatively straightforward operation, but in Jesus' time, she had spent all her money on treatment by doctors, suffering much at their hands, until as Luke (a doctor himself) records, no-one could heal her.

It was this woman who risked ridicule and punishment to reach out and touch Jesus. He did not dismiss her but, ignoring the religious and social customs, he pronounced her healed. 'Daughter, your faith has healed you. Go in peace.'

A deep strength

On 6th March 1986, Jill Saward experienced what every women fears and what no man can truly understand the effects of. The foreword of her courageous book states,

> At lunchtime on Thursday March 6th 1986, Jill Saward was viciously raped in her own home. Her father, the Reverend Michael Saward, Vicar of St Mary's, Ealing, and her boyfriend, David Kerr, were badly beaten. Jill was twenty-one and a virgin. The senseless violence of what came to be known as the Ealing Vicarage Rape Case shocked the nation. The light sentences handed out to the

rapists, partly because of what the judge saw as Jill's remarkable recovery from her trauma, shocked the nation all over again.[7]

It is a remarkable story – the first book by the victim of a rapist ever to be written. Parts of it are shocking, all of it is moving. Rape is often cited as the ultimate difference between men and women where the physical strength of the male species enables the woman to be manipulated, used and abused. For many feminists it is society in a microcosm. Jill Saward admits that her idea of men has changed since the attack and the subsequent trauma.

> My image of men has taken a beating. I've always thought of them as some kind of supermen. Strong. Able to do anything. Faced with weapons, the two who could have protected me had no more resources than I did ... I still see men as the protectors but I've come to realise that there are instances when I have more endurance and stamina than some men. Most of the men I know are weaker than me in many ways. Not physically maybe. It doesn't take much to flatten me, and I will still run from pain. I'm talking about the strength a person has in themselves.[8]

Jill Saward is a remarkable woman who has suffered much at the hands of some men, and at the words, written and spoken, of many. The way in which the incident was reported in the popular press added to her injuries and trauma. Yet despite the pain, anger and injustice which she rightly feels, there is too a deep strength which has enabled her to begin to

[7]Foreword to *Rape: My Story*, Jill Saward (Bloomsbury, 1990).
[8]*Rape: My Story*.

come to terms with what has happened to her. For some people this is difficult to understand, as was apparent in the words of the judge in his sentencing of Jill's attackers. He mistook her apparent recovery as evidence that she had suffered 'no great trauma' through the assault. He was wrong.

Jill's strength came from her deep Christian commitment, and her family and friends. For some women the fact that Jesus became a man is a barrier to their becoming Christians. For Jill, the Jesus of the gospels was to be a source of love, strength and acceptance in a way that no-one else could be. A woman abused by men found compassion and understanding from the only perfect man who has ever lived. She concludes her book with these astonishing words,

> All this has taught me in a special way that no one is beyond the scope of God's love. Some may never have known real security with people. Human relationships often fall short of our expectations. Without God I would not be here today . . . He was there when I was being attacked and no human person came to my aid. The joy I was able to experience after the rape was so supernatural it just said, 'Look. God is so much greater than you could expect. He'll carry you through the tough times.' He didn't leave me alone to get on with it. Whenever I recognised my need, He was in there with me, pouring out his love through others to me.

Both the woman in the gospel account and Jill Saward found healing and peace from Jesus. Both were in pain and sought relief from Jesus. Society and the church have been guilty, sadly, of causing pain to women through oppression and sexism. One of the tragedies of the modern church is that some women feel unable to stay within its walls and confines. In rejecting the church, some feel compelled to reject the church's founder at the same time. To do so, however, is to misunderstand the life, death and teaching of Jesus. He was born a man but it is as the supreme example of humanity that he shows us how to live life God's way. Through his coming, he gave humanity – male and female – the possibility of knowing God. He did not come simply for Jews but for the whole world, irrespective of gender, colour, race or religion. He came for people of all types and personalities. The famous and the unknown have found meaning, healing and purpose through a relationship with him. Women of faith have been instrumental in the growth and development of the church, and before. It was to women that Jesus first appeared following his resurrection. It is women that have often been the mainstays of faith throughout the history of Christianity. The way the church has misused and abused women is all the more marked when compared with the attitude of Jesus to women. They did not simply make the connection with Jesus – he made the connection with them. He met them where they were, in their pain and rejection and has continued to do so ever since. The offer still stands.

For more information

Rape: My Story, Jill Saward (Bloomsbury, 1990).
Split Image, Ann Atkins (Hodder & Stoughton Ltd, 1987).
Mark 5:22–43; Luke 8:41–56.

8

Living made sense

'**I** have had few difficulties, many friends, great successes. I have gone from wife to wife, from house to house and have visited the great countries of the world. But I am fed up with finding devices to fill up the 24 hours of the day.' So Ralph Barton, the cartoonist, summed up his life.

The psychiatrist Paul Walker was asked how he would describe the modern age. He said, 'For me, the key word is emptiness.'

The philosopher H. L. Mencken wrote, 'The basic fact about human experience is not that it is a tragedy but that it is a bore. It is not that it is predominantly painful, but that it is lacking any sense.'

The basic question of the meaning of life has occupied numerous thinkers, writers, broadcasters and has taken up much time on television and radio. Sigmund Freud reckoned that to even question the meaning of life was the act of a sick person. A whole school of French philosophers took a great deal of time to discover that life was meaningless. Jean-Paul Sartre reckoned that, 'Mankind is a mere puddle for whom freedom is death.' His fellow existentialist, Albert

Camus, concluded, 'It was previously a question of finding out whether or not life had to have a meaning to be lived. It now becomes clear, on the contrary, that it will be lived all the better if it has no meaning.'

The question is: *are they right*? Does it matter? Our society is one that is based on tolerance. Mutual understanding and communication are encouraged, extremists are not. People who claim to be 'right' are pilloried as being narrow-minded, but only if they disagree with our point of view! With the question of the meaning of life, however, it does matter who is right and who is wrong.

Unlike supporting a football team or choosing whether to shop at Marks and Spencers or Debenhams, it is not a question of personal choice only. Jesus said some things that were either true or false.

1. True or false?: 'I am the way and the truth and the life. No-one comes to the Father except through me' (John 14:6).

2. True or false?: 'I am the resurrection and the life. He who believes in me will live, even though he dies; and whoever lives and believes in me will never die' (John 11:25–26).

3. True or false?: 'Anyone who has seen me has seen the Father' (John 14:9).

4. True or false?: 'I have come that they may have life, and have it to the full' (John 10:10).

These statements are either correct or hopelessly wrong. Christianity is either true or false. There is no room for saying that Jesus was partially correct. Neither can a decision be made on what seems right or how it feels. Any reasonable decision on the claims of Jesus must surely be made on the facts. Sadly too the church has not often presented the Christian faith in a way that has been meaningful, understandable and relevant. We all have had bad experiences in church services that seemed boring or never-ending. There are many churches where the faith of those leading, and those attending, must be in doubt as the teaching and results are so far removed from the faith found in the pages of the New Testament. Many of us can agree with Camus when he wrote, 'The church has offered to introduce us to God. But when we accept the invitation and arrive at the royal palace, we see protocol, pomp and circumstance, business, buildings, plans and programmes, but the king is not there.'

So, if feelings, the way society thinks and even parts of the church(!) have to be disregarded, how can you make up your mind?

In the course of this book, we have examined various parts of our society's make-up, and some possible explanations and remedies. Money, love and death have all come under the microscope. The Christ of the gospels has something to say to each of these situations, and the people in them. However, the most powerful demonstration of who Jesus is came, ironically, at the end of his life. If we look at John's Gospel, for instance, well over half of his book is taken up with the death of Jesus, and the days leading up to it. So why was the death of Jesus so important? Was it a mistake?

We have already seen how committed Jesus was to humanity. That he was prepared to die was perhaps the ultimate identification of God with people. But is that all it is? An example to us of how we should die?

No, clearly if it was that significant to occupy over half of John's Gospel, and several sections of the other historical accounts of the life of Jesus, it must be more important.

We've seen too how the opponents of Jesus, when he was alive and since, recognized that he was a 'good man'. So how did this good man come to die at such an early age, innocent of any crime, not tried by any valid court, and with unreliable witnesses speaking against him? His means of death was perhaps the cruellest that humanity has ever devised. Again, rather like the question as to who Jesus really was, it is best to see how he saw his own death, in his own words.

In the account of Jesus' life given to us by a doctor, Luke, there is a description of two incidents that can tell us a lot about how Jesus viewed his death. In the ninth chapter, we have what is known as 'Peter's confession'. Now this wasn't a catalogue of everything that Peter, one of the disciples, had done wrong – a sort of *News of the World* exposé! On the contrary, Peter got something right for once. Having been with Jesus for two years, the penny finally drops. Jesus asks his disciples who they think he is.

Peter replies, 'You are the Christ, the Son of the Living God' (verse 20). The word 'Christ' means 'Messiah' or 'Anointed One'. This was the person that the Jews had been waiting for – God's special messenger and rescue agent. Jesus' reaction to Peter's announcement is at first puzzling. He warns them not to tell anyone about it, and then goes on to tell them that he must die. Why? The clue comes in the second incident described for us by Luke.

About a week later, Jesus took three of his close friends on a walking trip. They went up a mountain with Jesus to pray. A quite remarkable event took place. The disciples, as usual, fell asleep while Jesus was praying. Suddenly they awoke to find an incredible scene in front of them. Jesus' face had become changed in some way and his clothes shone like lightning. Hard to believe? Perhaps, but we have no reason to doubt the three witnesses. They saw Jesus talking to two people, Moses and Elijah. Hang on, you say, weren't they dead? Well, yes they were, physically. But if God came into this world, crossing over from eternity into time, isn't it possible for that same God to pass back into eternity, now and again?

The subject of their conversation is of prime interest to

us, however. Moses, the great symbol of the Old Testament Law (God's guidelines for living), and Elijah, the representative of the Old Testament prophets (God's spokespersons to his people), talked with Jesus about his 'departure' – his death! You see, his death was no accident. It was planned in heaven. Why? Again, the words of Jesus himself are the biggest help to us. Only this time, we'll examine the very words that Jesus said while he was on the cross itself.

1. 'Father, forgive them, for they do not know what they are doing' (Luke 23:34)

Jesus had been arrested, whipped, beaten up and abused. The Romans were experts in torture and pain. The whipping itself was often enough to bring about the death of the prisoner. They were so good at it that if they wanted to, they could remove the skin off a man's back, his entrails and still leave him alive. Crucifixion was one of the slowest and most painful forms of execution ever devised by humanity. And yet, at the height of the agony of the pain and suffering, these remarkable words were heard to come from the mouth of Jesus. Forgiveness is at the heart of the Christian faith. The message of Christianity is that forgiveness is possible. God can, and will, forgive people. People like you and me. He is not a God with a big stick, waiting to hit people and to punish them. He is a God of love and compassion. But how is this forgiveness achieved? Does God simply let us off for all the wrong things we do, say and think? No, he doesn't. The clue lies in the next words of Jesus on the cross.

2. My God, my God, why have you forsaken me?' (Mark 15:34)

These are, at first sight, very strange words. There is an eerie feel to them for many people. Difficult to understand, yet so easy to relate to. Facing death, it is surely natural to cry out at God in anger and bitterness, 'Why have you let this happen to me?' For Jesus, there is surely even more reason. Why should God forsake his own Son, at this, his time of greatest need. To understand what was happening here, we have to see it in the wider context of the teaching of the whole Bible. We have seen that God is a God of compassion and love, and a God who wants to forgive us. In tension with this, however, is the fact that God is also a God of justice and perfection. Now for justice to be done in a court of law, some punishment has to be given if the accused is found guilty. Otherwise, it would not be justice. Imagine the outcry if a convicted murderer was let off scot-free! We saw earlier how each one of us has failed to come up to God's standards for our lives. Therefore, we should be punished. It would not be the act of a just God to let us all off. But because God's justice is in tension with his love, he sent Jesus.

He did come up to God's standard of perfection. He lived a perfect life because of who he was – God and humanity in perfect harmony. Yet because of this perfection, he was the only one who was acceptable to God; the only one who was good enough, brave enough and morally and physically tough enough to accept punishment on our behalf. He was punished for our failures. The extent of God's concern and love for the world can be seen in the way he entered its suffering, pain and alienation in the person of Jesus. In a way that we'll never fully understand Jesus gave up his life willingly, out of obedience to the Father. That obedience cost him his life but bought life for all of us.

The cry of Jesus came as he experienced a separation from God that he'd never known before. We know it all the time. We don't know anything different. But for Jesus, it was a new experience heightened by being punished for the failure of the whole world to reach God's pass mark. How long did it last and was it effective? The third and final clue tells us.

3. 'It is finished!' (John 19:30)

These words too have prompted much debate and controversy. Is it a cry of defeat or resignation? Relief perhaps that the agony is at an end? The word itself unravels the mystery. It is translated by the Greek word 'Tetalestai' which means 'It is finished', or literally, 'It is paid.' The Greek word would have been stamped across bills due in the ancient world. Imagine if your electricity or gas bill arrived next month with the word 'It is paid' written on it. You'd be pretty pleased!

That is an insight into what the final cry of Jesus means for you and me. It is a cry of victory, triumph and affirmation. It's like the end of the Cup Final at Wembley as the manager hugs his team: 'We've done it!'

Jesus has made it possible for you and me to be forgiven. By his separation from God on a wooden Roman gibbet 2,000 years ago, he has enabled you and me to make sense of life and death. The life of Jesus is remarkable. His teachings are remarkable. His death is out of this world! It has made it possible for you and me to begin a relationship with God, and to live our lives as they were meant to be lived. The past can be forgiven, the future faced with certainty. Even death itself need hold no fear. A relationship with God, through Jesus, gives us identity, peace and security in a world where all are rare. It enables us to make sense of our relationships in the family and beyond. The key to all of this is the death of Jesus Christ. So, have you begun to make the connection? If you don't think Jesus is who he claims to be, that he wasn't the Son of God and that he wasn't raised from the dead, then his death is insignificant. It is just one more statistic of the Roman Empire. It is history.

If, however, you do think he is who he claimed to be, then there are some implications that you and I have to face up to. We cannot ignore what he says about life, death and the promises he offers us. His death is not simply an event in history but an event that split history in two. Life and death were never meant to be the same. Indeed, he went further than that. The resurrection of Jesus was not the end of the story. His death split history, but his return will bring the past, present and future together. The next chapter examines this incredible prediction – that Jesus will return again.

For more information

The Empty Cross of Jesus, M. Green (Hodder & Stoughton Ltd, 1984)
The Trial of Jesus, Val Grieve (STL/IVP, 1990).
Luke 9:18–36.

9

New age or new kingdom

Just before Easter 1991 the world was astounded to learn that the Son of God had played football in England for Hereford United and Coventry City! The former professional footballer, journalist and official spokesperson for the Green Party, David Icke, stunned listening journalists by telling them that he was an aspect of the divine godhead, that he and his family originated from the planet Oereal in another solar system and that the world was heading towards an ecological disaster unparalleled in human history. The reaction, not surprisingly, was one of disbelief and ridicule. Embarking on the round of chat shows on radio and television to promote his ideals, he would appear dressed in a turquoise track suit, a colour harmonious with the vibrations of the planet. Some people thought it was a publicity stunt, while others questioned his sanity.

He resigned from his position with the Green Party and announced that, following several journeys in Canada and South America, he had been sent by the godhead to warn humanity of its predicament and fate. He announced that, conveniently, his wife and daughter were aspects of the archangel Michael, while he accused the church of having corrupted the real message that Jesus sought to communicate. His book *The Truth Vibrations* (published by Aquarian Press, 1991) sold extremely well, especially after several earthquakes and volcanic eruptions hit the headlines. But why was he taken so seriously? Why did the book sell so well? Was he insane, deluded or was he telling the truth, incredible as it might seem? In reality he was the tip of an iceberg. There were thousands of people who, although not agreeing with everything he said, held views not too dissimilar.

For example, what do the following have in common: a prostitute, a beheaded male court jester, a harem dancer, a monk, a Russian ballet dancer, a Brazilian voodoo practitioner, a Chinese tai-chi artist, and a teenager from Peru? Don't know? They are all, if we are to believe her, the previous incarnations of the American actress Shirley MacLaine. She has become a self-styled spokesperson for this new, and at the same time ancient, religious movement. It encompasses anything and everything – from acupuncture to Zen Buddhism, and Zodiac research to the Age of Aquarius. Although difficult to define precisely or sum up in a set of common beliefs, the 'New Age' or 'New Era' movement has crept slowly and subtly into many parts of the world. Most 'believers' agree that just as Jesus inaugurated the 'Age of Pisces' (the fish), a new 'age' was to be started – the Age of Aquarius.

Its roots are a combination of eastern religion coupled with western commercialism and realism. It embraces all religions and creeds, and those religions with no creed at all. Its followers are many and increasing in number. As Shirley MacLaine herself has written,

> They are individuals who are profoundly concerned with what is happening on our planet and ALL the life residing on it. New Agers include

antiwar activists, pro-environmentalists, anti-nukers, peaceniks, feminists, ecologists, bankers, psychologists, doctors, physicists, blue-, white- and even non-collar workers, and many, many more – so there are apparently millions of people who advocate the 'selfish' view of wanting to save our planet from destruction by beginning with themselves . . .[1]

The movement came to the notice of most people when, on 16 August 1987, 'Harmonic convergence' ceremonies were held at more than 350 sites across the world from Ayres Rock in Australia to Stonehenge in England, from the Great Pyramids of Egypt to the Chaco Canyon in New Mexico, USA. The aim was for 144,000 people to hum, chant, hug, dance and pray for world peace. Despite a vastly reduced attendance, the day was judged a success as, it was said, the Presidents of the USSR and USA met for a summit conference shortly afterwards. Elsewhere, other New Agers offered weekend courses in body harmony, aromatherapy, the study of the healing properties of crystals, management seminars in 'self-realization' techniques, and difficult children were sent to swim with dolphins because of their therapeutic qualities! Many bookshops contained large New Age/Era sections, while a New Era shop opened in Birmingham offering treatments from headache pills to tarot cards. But as someone asked me recently, 'What's wrong with what they believe? Surely their aims are the same as the church's?'

Their popularity is a sign, undoubtedly, of the fact that humanity has a spiritual side but is what they believe really the same as Christianity?

Firstly, most New Age belief is of the opinion that

[1]*Loving Within*, Shirley MacLaine (Bantam Books, 1990).

everything is on the same level. The chair you are sitting upon is as much a part of God and God is as much a part of it as you are. Shirley MacLaine again,

> Basic to New Age subatomic discoveries is the concept that in the subatomic world – the stuff of the universe – everything, every last thing, is linked. The universe is a gigantic, multidimensional web of influences, or information, light particles, energy patterns, and electromagnetic 'fields of reality'. Everything it is, everything we are, everything we do, is linked to everything else. There is no separateness . . . we are each Godlike and God is in each one of us . . . We are literally made up of God energy, therefore we can create whatever we want in life because we are each co-creating with the energy of God – the energy that makes the universe itself.

Unlike some religions, such as Christianity, Judaism and Islam, which see the world as a double-decker bus, the New Agers see the universe as a single decker. Everything is on the same level – you, me, this book and the chair you are sitting on. Although on the same level, however, there exist different dimensions. David Icke revealed that there are thirteen different ones. The different dimensions share the same space, however – they're just on different frequencies, a bit like different radio stations.

The second belief common to most of the New Age is that of reincarnation. It is not a new belief but is common to Hinduism and Buddhism. Basically, it is the belief that one goes from one life to another with the soul passing from one body to another, the slow inexorable progression of a spiritual evolution. It assumes the existence of 'karma' – that what we think and do (and don't think and do) sets into motion what occurs in our lives. One life is not long enough for this to be worked out, hence the need for another life. The belief in reincarnation angers some and depresses others. Woody Allen, with characteristic pessimism, reckoned that if he believed in reincarnation, he'd come back as a sponge! Sir Winston Churchill on the other hand asserted that, 'If, when I die, I find myself returned to this planet as a mouse, I would be unable to be anything other than extremely cross with the Almighty.'

But again, is it true and how do these beliefs fit in with what Jesus said, and did? Let's take the first one first.

In his best selling novel, *Stark*, Ben Elton pictured a world that is dying. The world is our world and the time – *now*! As more and more people realized the desperate plight of the environment, the book certainly hit a chord. In the story, a group of the richest men on earth buy themselves an escape from the dying planet – a spaceship that will enable them to live on the moon. But the dream goes wrong:

> The problem was not the conditions. It was not the work they had to do, nor even the food – the problem was the company. They had escaped pollution on earth, only to discover that they had carried with them another pollution that they could not escape. The pollution in their own souls.[2]

This is a realistic assessment of the state of humanity. The fact is that none of us feels a part of God – we are separated from God. We know that we are not the people we are meant to be. Even those religions which teach that God is 'within' recognize that there is a process to go through before one gets in touch with the divine within. Christianity

[2]*Stark*, Ben Elton (Martin Joseph, 1992).

clearly teaches that although made in the image of God, that image has been tarnished and damaged. We are not the people we were meant to be. The world around us is not how God intended it to be. The Christian faith calls this *sin*. But there is a clear distinction between humanity and the rest of creation. We have been given the ability to determine our own future. We feel our alienation from God and the guilt that arises from our failure and rebellion. As Mark Twain pointed out, a human being is the only animal that blushes! The New Age belief that everything contains a 'spark' of the divine or the vibrations of peace or the energy of love is in direct contradiction to the Christian faith.

Secondly, what about reincarnation? This too is in direct opposition to the teachings of Jesus which speak of resurrection *not* reincarnation. There are problems with trying to apply reincarnation to the events as described in the accounts of the life of Jesus. When he appeared to his disciples, following his resurrection, was he simply someone else reincarnated or was he on his way to another incarnation? When he raised Lazarus from the dead, from which incarnation was he bringing him back? Another objection is the attitude displayed by Jesus to the Old Testament. He clearly believed it to be true and to show the truth about life and death. Yet in the collection of prayers and hymns we call the Psalms, it outlines human life as spanning about seventy years and then finishing (Psalm 90:10). Reincarnation is not to be found anywhere in the Bible.

David Icke obviously believes in it, however, and so do many New Agers. Icke sees those people who suffer from mental and physical handicaps as being souls who deliberately choose to be handicapped in order to develop a part of their character and experience. They take the chance for one of their lives to live as a handicapped person. This helps them to develop as souls. Other tragedies are explainable too, according to Icke. A cot death can be understood in several ways. It might be a soul that changes its mind shortly after beginning its present incarnation. Or it might be the soul of an advanced spiritual teacher that leaves the body of a baby shortly after birth in order to challenge its parents with the lessons of overcoming their grief. I don't think even the most extreme do-gooder would dare to say this to a parent who had recently lost a baby in this way! Icke also believes that any evil done in an incarnation would be repaid in a later one. God, he says, does not judge but the 'spiritual law' naturally works out the implications for the future. Apparently a soul is neither male nor female, simply a divine 'spark' that inhabits a human body for a while!

But is our sin responsible for what happens to us in this life, and after death? Is suffering a punishment for not doing good? Are we really to believe that all those killed in earthquakes, air disasters and train crashes are being punished for evil done in past lives? Are there really no people who are innocent victims? Are we really to believe, as David Icke does, that the 250,000 people killed in a cyclone in Bangladesh died because they were never meant to live there? What does the Bible say about 'karma' or fate and its connection with suffering?

The problem of suffering and evil has always been a difficult one for anyone to explain. Yet the pain and suffering of much human existence demands some sort of response. There are several responses one can make, depending on one's point of view.

For the humanist, the random selection of certain victims in disasters leads to what amounts to a stoical acceptance, a shrug of the shoulders, a statement that 'That's life!' and conclusive evidence that God does *not* exist.

For some followers of Islam (*lit.* 'submission'), any mishap is simply the will of Allah. All evil comes from him as he shall choose. This was clearly demonstrated when, upon the death of hundreds of Muslim pilgrims to Mecca, an Islamic ruler declared that they would have died at that moment wherever they were, because it had obviously been the will of Allah.

For the Christian Scientist, it is a question of mind over matter. Pain can simply be imagined away. You may have heard the story of the Christian Scientist who told her friend that her husband imagined he was ill. A week later the friend inquired as to the husband's illness only to be told that the husband now imagined himself to have died.

For Hindus, as with New Agers, a person suffers what they deserve, while for the Buddhists the aim is 'Nirvana' (*lit.* 'blowing out'), the self-annihilation towards an existence of no pain, and indeed no existence.

But what of Christianity? What does it say to suffering and the problem of evil?

Firstly, it recognizes that it is not simply an academic discussion or theoretical problem. People throughout the centuries have experienced pain, bereavement, rejection, anger at injustice and rage at a world that does not seem to make any sense at all. In the face of this, the Christian claim that God is good, caring and just can seem trite and empty. Yet this *is* what is claimed. The disasters of our world, both natural and incidental, are a consequence of our failure to live up to God's standards and desires. The claim that there is a direct link between the behaviour of humanity and the problems of the planet is not the prerogative of the environmentalists. From the beginning of the account of how God deals with humanity, one of the consequences of humanity's rebellion against God's guidelines for living has been that the earth itself has been affected. In the language of Genesis, God 'cursed' the earth, following Adam and Eve's disobedience. In the New Testament, Paul sees creation as waiting for the perfection Jesus will bring in the future (Genesis 3:17; Romans 8:18–22). The Christian faith asserts that the creation itself has been corrupted by humanity's disease, hence its imperfections such as floods, earthquakes and drought. Other disasters are clearly the fault of humanity. The drunk driver, political terrorist and the mugger are not innocent victims, yet there are consequences to their actions. Some do not simply fail to live up to God's standards but actively decide to reject God's standards and desires. As C. S. Lewis has written, 'We are not merely imperfect creatures who need to grow, we are rebels who need to lay down our arms.'

But the question remains – why doesn't God intervene to stop the terrorist or prevent the car from running over the three-year-old child? Why doesn't he send rain to Ethiopia or the Sudan? Could it be, as those who believe in reincarnation claim, that it really is the effect of past evil that condemns some to suffering, and even death?

Jesus was once asked whether or not people who died in such incidents were more guilty than other people, and his response was definite! 'Those eighteen who died when the tower in Siloam fell on them – do you think they were more guilty than all the others living in Jerusalem? I tell you, no!' (Luke 13:4).

Jesus was in no doubt that suffering is *not* a punishment for evil. There may sometimes be consequences to our actions. For example, if a driver drinks too much, it increases the possibility of an accident in the same way that if we put our hand in a fire, we will get burnt. But it is not as a result of evil done in previous lives or reincarnations. It may be a consequence of our failure or disregard for God's guidelines for our lives, but it is not a 'tit-for-tat' revenge situation!

So why doesn't God step in and prevent the terrorists' bomb from going off or move the steering wheel of the drunk's car? The answer may seem strange, and at first glance, almost cruel. He doesn't intervene in every situation because he loves us.

Now, to the mother of a six-month-old baby, diagnosed as having cancer, this would seem a strange way of God showing his love. But, if God were to step in and remove those responsible, then the outlook would be decidedly bleak for the entire human race. Because, if we all fail to live up to God's standards, then those responsible are you and me! All of us would be removed from the scene, or at least become mere puppets in the hands of a God that is unrecognizable as the God of the Bible.

Yet, God has not stayed remote. He has come in the person of Jesus and felt injustice, cruelty, anger, frustration, sorrow, grief and pain. But Jesus himself used the question of suffering as a platform to warn people as to the future. He spoke of a future when he would return – of a new kingdom, rather than a new age.

But what will this kingdom be like, and when will it begin? Briefly . . .

a. The things that appear permanent are actually passing and transient

This is one of the ways in which the New Age movement appears to be similar to Christianity yet is totally different. Jesus said he would return and when he did, things would be different. Why should we believe him? Well, it is estimated that over 360 Old Testament prophecies came true in the birth, life, death and resurrection of Jesus and the chances of that occurring in another individual's life are 1:10,000,000,000,000,000,000,000,000,000,000.

b. Before Jesus comes again, there will be many people who will claim to be him

Jesus himself predicted this – he told his disciples, 'For many will come in my name, claiming, "I am the Christ," and will deceive many . . . For false Christs and false prophets will appear and perform great signs and miracles'

(Matthew 24:5, 24). Since 19 July 1977 adverts have appeared declaring *'The Christ is now here.'* The Lord Maitreya is said to be the new Christ and will appear at any time. We're still waiting! David Icke was not the first and will not be the last to claim to be the Son of God. When Jesus comes again he will not be appearing on any chat shows.

c. The second coming of Jesus will mark the end and fulfilment of history

As someone put it, 'When Jesus returns, that's it – the play's over. It's as if the author has walked onto the stage and wound up the production. No curtain calls, no repeat performance – that's it, the finish.' Unlike his first coming as a fragile baby in an obscure backwater of the Roman Empire, his second coming will be such that it will leave no-one in any doubt as to his identity and authority. He pictured it thus, 'They will see the Son of Man coming on the clouds of the sky, with power and great glory' (Matthew 24:30).

d. The kingdom that will be initiated will be one where there is no pain, sadness, grief, injury, injustice or tragedy

As one of the Bible writers puts it, 'He will wipe every tear from their eyes. There will be no more death or mourning or crying or pain, for the old order of things has passed away' (Revelation 21:4).

e. The coming of the new kingdom will mean all of us coming face to face with God

We *will* all be judged according to how we have reacted to Jesus, and how we have lived. Our response to Jesus is our response to God, and in making our minds up about him, we decide our own fate beyond death. We will not decide what reincarnation we assume but whether we go to be with God for ever – to heaven. It could be said that God simply underlines our choice. The alternative is to live without God for ever – hell. This cannot be avoided, however unpalatable an idea it might be.

As C. S. Lewis has said, 'The Christian faith presents us with a God so full of mercy that he becomes a man and dies by torture to avert that final ruin for his creatures, and who yet, where that heroic remedy fails, seems unwilling or even unable, to arrest the ruin by an act of mere power . . . And here is the problem: so much mercy, yet still there is a hell.'

That is the reality of what happens after death. No reincarnation as a frog, beetle or even another human being, but a resurrection to either life or death. The choice is ours – heaven or hell, life or death. Jesus is the one who holds the answers to life and death, and to the new age or kingdom. Anybody else is merely making an educated guess or sharing their vain optimism. The one who suffered for our sake is the one who will put an end to suffering. His suffering, as we described in the previous chapter, enables us to begin a relationship with God. The next chapter outlines how you can do that.

For more information

Read Matthew 24.
The Pilgrim's Guide to the New Age, Alice and Stephen Lawhead (Lion, 1986).
Understanding the New Age, Russell Chandler (Word, 1989).
The Problem of Pain, C. S. Lewis (Collins, 1940).

10

This is it!

Any relationship has to have a beginning. Remember your first boyfriend or girlfriend? It was difficult to know what to say at first. The shy looks, nervous glances and stuttered 'Hellos'. It can be hard to know what to do or say. You're afraid of saying or doing the wrong thing so you behave as you think you should. Chocolates are bought, perfume sprayed and flowers purchased. Slowly, as the friendship develops, the real you emerges! Not quite like a butterfly, more like a chrysalis! But if the relationship is to last, the pretence must stop. The relationship will probably mean that you don't stay the same, either of you.

Beginning a relationship with God can be very similar. There are the things that people do that are expected of them – like going to church, praying and so on. Some of them are helpful, some not so. Here are some hints.

a. Be yourself!
God made you and literally 'broke the mould'. There is no-one else who is exactly like you. You are unique. That doesn't stop now you want to be a follower of Jesus. There

are certain things it will be helpful for you to do, but remember Christianity isn't a religion of rules and regulations. God accepts you as you are, although he wants to change you.

b. Start to find out from other people how they began the relationship

No doubt, some years ago, your parents sat you down for a chat. They were more embarrassed than you as they tried to explain what is euphemistically known as 'the Birds and the Bees'. Unknown to them you already knew all that they tried to tell you, and more besides! But, consciously or otherwise, we do learn from others how to conduct a friendship. It can be helpful to read about how other people have begun a relationship with God, and the difference it has made to their lives.

Better still, ask people you know how they began their Christian life. I guarantee none of them will be the same!

c. Respond to the first move

God has made the first move to us in Jesus by coming, living and dying on the cross. It is up to us now to respond. How do you do this? Well, you have already begun. By reading this book, and getting this far, you have begun to respond. However, there is obviously all the difference between knowing about a relationship and actually being in one. You have to enter into a relationship with God. How do you do that? Simply, by talking to him.

d. Talk to each other

It would be a pretty funny relationship where no-one talked to each other. Such relationships do exist but they usually don't last very long! Parents usually know when a relationship is beginning because the phone bill suddenly increases. But, what do you say?

The religious word for this is prayer. Most people regard prayer as reeling off a shopping-list of things they want from God. It is for when everything else has failed or just before an exam or job interview. Can you imagine a marriage where all the husband and wife say to each other is what they want from the other one or where they only talk to each other as a last resort? Communication is integral to a relationship – listening as well as talking to each other. Make time to listen to God as well as telling him what you're worried about, what you dream of and what you'd like to happen. Above all, be yourself. He wants a relationship with you, not a religious nut-case! But real prayer will change things – us, the way we look at the world around us and the way we behave towards one another. Prayer involves seeing ourselves, other people and the world around us as God sees them.

e. Repair the relationship

We were always meant to have a relationship with God. It is not his fault that things are as they are. It's ours. So, we have to begin the relationship by saying sorry. This is very often the first prayer that people say to God when beginning a relationship with him. The film *Love Story* gave birth to the following saying: 'Love means never having to say you're sorry.' Most relationships, even the most loving ones, cannot survive on that basis. The one we have with God is no different. We need to say we are sorry.

f. The first meeting

The most important thing on a first meeting is usually having enough to say, or knowing the right thing to say! So what do you say to God? There are three important things to recognize in such a prayer.

First, that you have failed to come up to God's standards, are sorry, and want to begin to live life God's way.

Second, to recognize who Jesus is and what he accomplished in his life and on the cross.

Third, to ask for the forgiveness possible through Jesus, to ask God's help to live for him, and to ask him to be with you for ever. Such a prayer is set out below. You can make it your own prayer by saying it to God and so beginning a relationship with him.

> Thank you Jesus for coming into this world
>
> I recognize my failure to live up to your standards, the things I have done, said and thought. I admit my sin to you, and ask you to forgive me for it.
>
> Thank you Jesus for dying on the cross that I might be forgiven, for being rejected that I might be accepted and for being separated from your Father than I might be re-united with him. Thank you for your willingness to die for me. I acknowledge you as my Saviour and my God.
>
> Please forgive me and come in to my life now.
>
> I want to live for you from now on, to do the things that please you, and show you that I love you.
>
> Please help me to live for you and fill me with your love and strength.
>
> Thank you Lord Jesus. Amen.

('Amen' is simply a religious way of saying, 'Yes – I really agree with that!')

It isn't always easy to begin a relationship. Beginning a friendship with God is harder than most. Other people often find it hard to understand and think we're stupid, or weak. Don't be put off. Jesus was prepared to suffer, to endure pain and go through agony that your friendship with him might come about. He thought you were worth it.

So, where do you go from here?

Although it is not a relationship of rules, there are certain things that it is helpful to do, and others that aren't. It would be a strange marriage if the couple didn't share the same house. Similarly, a girlfriend would not look too kindly on a boy who never talked to her or met with her. So:

a. Meet with God with others

I can hear several people saying, 'Here it comes – the church plug!' Well, yes, here it is, but for a good reason. It can be very hard being a follower of Jesus in today's society. It has always been difficult. In today's society, however, there are particular pressures on people who become Christians. So, what could be more encouraging than to meet with people that share your beliefs and know how you feel? Meeting people who are more experienced than you and who have perhaps been through some of the same experiences can help.

Also, in any relationship, it is vital that love is expressed. The same applies to your relationship with God and his with you. The word for 'worship' in Hebrew means literally 'to draw near to kiss'. In essence, that is what is happening in a church service. We tell God that we love him through hymns, songs and prayers. At the same time we are reminded of his love for us through the songs and readings from the Bible. We are reminded of what it cost God to enable us to have a relationship with us as we eat the bread and drink the wine in a communion service as we remember Jesus' death and resurrection. It is vital, therefore, that we meet with other Christians to worship God, hear more about him and be encouraged in our relationship with him.

In beginning a relationship with God, you have entered a family that is called the church. Just like your own family, you couldn't choose them and they couldn't choose you. They will have faults, and believe it or not, so do you! Be patient!

b. Meet with God by yourself

It is, however, *your* relationship with God. So it is vital that you talk to God regularly by yourself. If you can, set aside a special time each day to spend with God. It might be first thing in the morning, in your lunch hour or late at night. Do this as well as talking to God all through the day.

c. Meet with God through the Bible

The Bible is a quite remarkable book. In it there is history, poetry, prophecy, guidelines for living, and the historical accounts of the life of Jesus. *Do* start to read it. *Don't* start with Genesis! Begin with one of the gospels. There are some aids on reading the Bible and a list is at the end of this chapter. Do get one as the Bible is not a simple book to understand. Buy a translation such as the New International Version or the New Revised Standard Version. These versions are easier to read.

d. Meet with God through joining the church

Most relationships reach a stage when those involved want to 'go public'. We call this marriage! A relationship with God is no different. Churches do differ about how they view membership. All encourage water baptism if you haven't been baptised before. If you have, then some churches encourage you to confirm those promises yourself, while others will encourage you to be baptised again. When you have found a church that you feel happy in, ask the minister or leader about baptism.

e. Meet with God through his Spirit

Now you have begun a relationship with God, he doesn't just leave you alone and say, 'See you in sixty years' time. Have a nice time and do your best!' God promises to be with us and the way he is present with us is through his Spirit. The Holy Spirit is given to us to help us and to make us more like Jesus. We need God's help every day if we are going to live for him. Make a point of asking God to be with you in all you do and say. When you have prayed a prayer like the one above, you might like to pray another one like this, today and every day.

Thank you, Lord Jesus, for beginning a relationship with me.
I ask now that you would come and give me more
of yourself.
Please fill me with your Holy Spirit,
that I might become more like Jesus.

Thank you for this lovely gift of your Spirit,
and for your love for me.
Amen.

As in any relationship, there are things to discover about each other and that process of discovery never ends. So it is with God. You'll discover more and more of God's love for you, and begin to understand things that puzzle you at the moment. It won't always be easy but it is worth it. We have God's promise on that.

Bob Geldof brought life to millions because he saw a need and responded to it. Hopefully, through reading this book, you will have seen that we all need to have life brought to us; life as it was meant to be. Millions have found that life. They made the connection between Jesus and themselves, realizing that Jesus made the connection possible between humanity and God. I hope you have made the connection yourself. The offer of life still rings true.

'I have come that they might have life and have it in all its fulness' (John 10:10).

Some helpful books

Scripture Union publish helpful Bible notes called 'Meeting Jesus'. You can buy them from most Christian bookshops or ask a friend to get one for you.

The Fight, John White (IVP, 1977). This book covers several major issues and subjects and is a most helpful book for new Christians.

It Makes Sense, Steve Gaukroger (Scripture Union, 1987). This is a book that covers most of the arguments against Christianity. You will find it helpful for yourself and to give away.

Too Busy Not to Pray, Bill Hybels (IVP, 1989). A comprehensive look at prayer and its importance.

Discipleship, David Watson (Hodder & Stoughton, 1983). As you grow as a Christian, you will find this book very helpful. It will help you deepen your relationship with God and answer many questions. Buy *The Fight* first however!

The God Book
Much more than a
role-play game
CHARLES and PETA SHERLOCK

You didn't plan it this way – but it's happened
all the same. Now that she's gone what are you
going to do next? Phone your brother Pete and
talk about what's happened? Take a drink and
forget about it all? Or think about where she
might possibly have gone?

Taking a highly successful idea from general
market role-play books, *The God Book* is a fresh
and original presentation of the Christian
message for young adults who read few Christian
books. It allows the reader to decide which page
to turn to next and so avoids the feeling that
'someone is telling us what to believe'.

Written in everyday language, this valuable new
evangelistic tool will be welcome by many as
another FRAMEWORKS book which explains
Christian truth in an enjoyable and down-to-
earth way.

96 pages   *Pocketbook*

FRAMEWORKS

How to Make the World Less Hungry

KATHY KEAY

A powerful and pictorial documentary designed to take God's concern for the world beyond those who read traditional 'missionary' books.

Moving from physical to spiritual hunger it introduces the problems of poverty and the various attempts to overcome them. Advice is given on handling the horrors shown on television and the constant call from major charities for support. Practical ideas are offered to show how everyone can make a difference and start to be involved with God's love in action.

How to Make the World Less Hungry is supported by TEAR Fund.

96 pages   *'B' format*

FRAMEWORKS

If I'm Honest

TIM STAFFORD and
PHILIP YANCEY

Two phrases current in youth culture are 'No
worries', said with an Australian accent, and
'Don't worry, be happy', a line from a recent
chart record.

Although Christians can know the truth of these
popular sayings, they are, in all honesty, far
away from the experience of many young adults
trying to be sincere in following Christ. After all,
the Christian life is no pushover and we all
acknowledge that we find some aspects deeply
troubling.

From temptation to suffering and legalism to
guilt, *If I'm Honest* explores common problems
of discipleship which do have answers. This is a
book for young adult Christians that goes
beyond the superficiality of a faith which
presents itself with a false smile.

96 pages   *'B' format*

FRAMEWORKS

Too Busy Not To Pray
Slowing down to be with God
BILL HYBELS

"For many years", confesses Bill Hybels, "I knew more about prayer than I ever practised."

Does that sound familiar? Most of us feel a niggling guilt at not 'praying enough'. Prayer takes time and stillness – and we're so busy!

Bill Hybels found a way out, "I did something absolutely radical," he says, "I prayed."

Now he shares what prompted him to take that life-changing step, and how you too can embark on the same adventure.

Bill Hybels is Senior Pastor of Willow Creek Community Church, South Barrington, Illinois.

160 pages   *Pocketbook*

Inter-Varsity Press

The Fight

JOHN WHITE

John White has written this book because he wants you to understand clearly what the Christian life is all about. He wants you to learn in the depths of your being that the eternal God loves you and plans only your highest good – more trust in him, more likeness to him.

But his love will bring pain as intense as your joy. For the Christian life is a fight....

"Reading *The Fight* is to inhale great draughts of fresh air into one's Christian life... This is the kind of book every 20th Century Christian should have on his book shelf."

Christian Weekly Newspapers

230 pages   Pocketbook

Inter-Varsity Press